Module 1
Lifestyle

1 My life

LEARNING AIMS

- Can discuss routines and habits
- Can use adverbs of frequency
- Can discuss daily activities

Lead-in

1 Look at the chart showing how Rachel spends each hour of her time in a typical week. Discuss the questions.

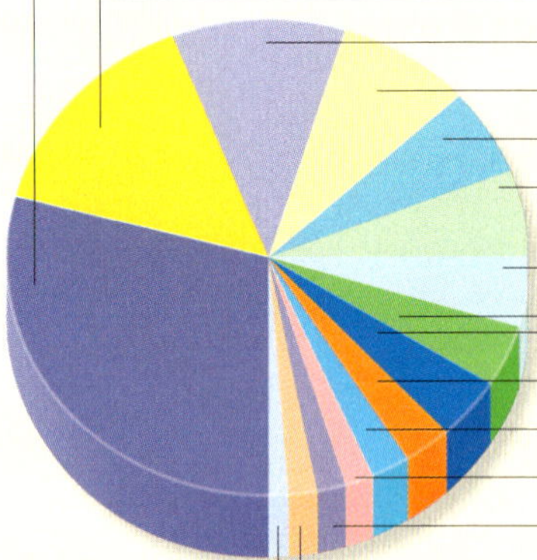

1. Does Rachel work, or is she a student?
2. What does she like doing most in her free time?
3. Is Rachel a sporty person, or more of a 'couch potato' – always sitting in front of the TV?
4. Does she have any hobbies?
5. How is her lifestyle similar to and different from yours?

2 Draw a chart similar to Rachel's. Include the activities in Rachel's chart and any other hobbies or activities that you do.

3 Work with a partner and discuss your charts. What do you like or dislike about your typical week? How would you like it to be different?

Reading and vocabulary

1 You are going to read an article about Vladimir Kramnik, a world champion chess player. Work with a partner and predict five ways that his life changed when he became world champion.

2 **01** Read the magazine article on page 3 and check your predictions.

3 Match these headings to the paragraphs in the text.

a Dealing with the media ☐
b Getting ready for a match ☐
c Relaxing after a match ☐
d Spending money ☐
e Starting my day ☐

4 Are these statements about Vladimir true or false?

1. Breakfast is an important meal for him. It helps to make him feel fresh. ☐
2. He doesn't spend much money on himself. ☐
3. Now he's champion he's got more time during the day to practise. ☐
4. He feels that the best way to improve is by playing games with other people. ☐
5. He goes to bed late because he needs time to relax after a tournament. ☐

5 Find words and phrases in the text which mean:

1 no value or reason (paragraph 1) ________________
2 pleasant and not too strong (paragraph 2) ________________
3 one after another (paragraph 3) ________________
4 the person you are playing against in a match (paragraph 4) ________________
5 a series of matches which shows who is the strongest player (paragraph 5) ________________
6 to begin to relax after a tense situation (paragraph 5) ________________

A life in the day of ...

1 It's quite difficult for me to get up in the morning. I like to lie in bed for ten minutes and think of nothing – it's my favourite ten minutes of the day. I don't get out of bed much before noon. There's no point in having a proper breakfast, I sometimes have just a cup of coffee, as lunch is at three o'clock. It's two hours before I feel completely fresh.

2 I don't care much about money. I've been a millionaire since my world championship with Kasparov, but I live like an ordinary Russian citizen. I don't have any special hobbies, like buying designer clothes or Ferraris. I have one luxury. I like caviar. Who doesn't? But if you eat it daily, you don't appreciate its delicate taste, so I eat it every other day! I like having money, but mainly so that I can help my family.

3 Since I became world champion, I get too many phone calls. Whether it's journalists or tournament organisers, it all takes time out of my day. A year ago I could read a book for two hours – now I don't even have two hours in a row free – more like 15 minutes. Everybody wants to speak to me. I've got four mobile phones, one that works around the world and three that work in Russia.

4 Being the world chess champion is a bit different from being the tennis champion. You don't need to practise chess to play well. It's more like scientific research. Preparation in chess is far more about thinking what your opponent will play. There are now more than two million chess games on the Internet. So I often study games and analyse them. I need to know what kind of openings and strategies my opponents are using.

5 I usually go to bed at 4 am. Almost all the chess players do. It's because chess tournaments don't finish until 10 pm. You can't go straight to bed after that. You need to unwind. You need to eat dinner, take a little walk and work on how to improve your game. Chess is intensive mental work. The last match I played against Kasparov went on for about a month, and I dreamt about chess every night. I was trying to solve chess problems in my dreams. Chess is like that.

Source: *A Life in the Day* by Richard Johnson for *The Sunday Times Magazine*

Speaking

1 Work with a partner. Look at these words and numbers from the text and discuss the importance they have in Vladimir's life.

the Internet	caviar	4 am	noon	10	mobile phone

2 Would you like to lead a lifestyle like Vladimir's?

3 Make a list of six words or numbers that reflect your own lifestyle.

4 Work with a partner. Exchange lists and guess what your partner's lists describe. How accurate were your guesses?

LANGUAGE STUDY

Routines and habits

1 Look at these sentences. Which two describe routines and habits? Which tense is used to talk about routines and habits?

a *I like to lie in my bed for ten minutes and think of nothing.*
b *I've been a millionaire since my world championship match.*
c *The last match I played went on for about a month.*
d *I don't get out of bed much before noon.*

2 We often add an adverb of frequency when we talk about routines and habits. Which word is the adverb of frequency in this sentence?

I sometimes have a cup of coffee.

3 Adverbs of frequency usually come between the subject and the main verb (except with the verb *be* when they come after the verb). Find two more examples of this in paragraphs 4 and 5 of the text on page 3.

4 Some adverbs of frequency can also be put at the beginning or end of sentences. This changes the emphasis. Look at these sentences and complete the rules.

Sometimes I work at weekends.
Often I don't have time to eat breakfast.
I never work late in the evenings.
He always checks his emails in the morning.
She speaks to me in French usually.
Occasionally I wake up before seven o'clock.
I am often too tired to cook when I get home.

1 The words *sometimes*, ___________ , ___________ and ___________ can be found at the beginning or end of sentences.

2 *Never* and ___________ are not normally found at the beginning or end of sentences.

Grammar reference page 26

5 Work with a partner. Make a list of adverbs of frequency and put them in order of frequency.

6 Add an adverb of frequency to these sentences so that they are true for you. Be honest!

Example: Between meals I eat snacks.
Between meals I sometimes eat snacks.

1 I am calm before exams.
2 I gossip about other people.
3 I ask people before I borrow their things.
4 I arrive at the station or bus stop with plenty of time before I catch trains or buses.
5 I tell people when I notice that they have food in their teeth.
6 I give up my seat for old people on public transport.
7 I tell my friend when he / she looks bad in an outfit.
8 I switch my mobile off before my English class.

Speaking **1** Work with a partner. Study the table and say six sentences about yourself.

			whenever possible	
	go to the cinema			
	go on holiday	less than	once	a day
I	read magazines	at least	twice	a week
	do the cooking	about	three times	a month
	use my mobile	more than	four times	a year
	visit my relatives			
			every day	

The lie-detector game

2 Write three sentences about your routines and habits. At least one of the statements must be true and at least one must be false. Try to think of unusual things that you do.

3 Work in groups. Take it in turns to ask questions about each person's statements.

Example:
A: *I go jogging at least four times a week.*
B: *How many kilometres do you jog?*
A: *About five.*
C: *How long does it take?*

4 For each person, guess which statements are true and which are false.

A new start

Listening and writing

1 Look at these pictures of a health farm. What do you think a health farm is? What do people do there? In what ways is it a 'new start'?

2 **02** Jenny is spending ten days at a health farm. She's already been there for a week and she's phoning her best friend Sarah to talk about her experience. Listen to the conversation and answer these questions.

1 What's her impression of the health farm?
2 What time does she get up?
3 What does she do before breakfast?
4 What does she do before lunch?
5 What does she eat for lunch?
6 How does she describe her health?

3 Work with a partner. You are going to write a leaflet for a short course at a health farm. Plan your writing. Decide:

- A name for your health farm and where it is
- What the timetable is for each day
- What food your guests eat
- What exercise your guests do on the course
- What activities the guests can and can't do in their free time
- Why the course is good for them
- How much the course costs and how to contact you

4 Write your leaflet. Include the information in Ex 3.

5 Present the details of your course to the class. Vote for the best course.

CD-ROM For more activities go to **Lifestyle Unit 1**

2 Who needs fame?

LEARNING AIMS

- Can sequence events
- Can discuss celebrity and privacy
- Can identify correct word stress

Lead-in

1 What are these people famous for? Make a list of their occupations.

Beethoven	Venus Williams	Leonardo da Vinci	Jackie Chan
Quentin Tarantino	Jennifer Lopez	Donatella Versace	Rudolf Nureyev
Michael Schumacher	Ronaldinho Gaucho		

Listening and vocabulary

1 Work with a partner. Make a list of the advantages and disadvantages of being famous.

2 03 Listen to a journalist talking about fame. Make a list of the four advantages and disadvantages of fame that she describes.

3 Compare your answers with a partner.

4 Explain the meanings of these phrases from the interview. Check your answers in Listening script 03 on page 30.

1. the top of their tree
2. live up to the expectations of the public
3. breaking up
4. suffer from low self-esteem
5. bullied at school
6. terrific drive to succeed

5 Do you know of any famous couples that have broken up this year? Do you know anyone who has a terrific drive to succeed? Have you ever seen a film that didn't live up to your expectations? Which film?

Word stress

Pronunciation

1 Put the words in the box into two lists – words with two syllables and words with three syllables.

advantage article exciting famous journalist magazine pressure privacy public terrific worry

2 04 Listen and underline the stressed syllable in each word in Ex 1.

Example: *advantage*

3 Read the rules and complete the examples using the words in Ex 1.

1. In words ending in *-ist*, *-phy*, *-cy* and *-gy* the stress is normally on the third syllable from the end. Examples: *privacy*, ____________
2. In words ending in *-ic* the stress is on the second last syllable. Examples: *public*, ____________
3. In most two-syllable words, the stress is on the first syllable. Examples: *worry*, ____________, ____________

Reading

1 Match these words from the magazine article to the definitions.

1	airborne	a	a court case
2	runway	b	get away from an unpleasant situation
3	achievement	c	taken prisoner, usually for money
4	kidnapped	d	moving or carried in the air
5	trial	e	a long road used by planes to take off from
6	escape	f	something done successfully

2 Look at the photos and the vocabulary in Ex 1. Predict what the article is about and what Charles Lindbergh was famous for.

3 **05** Read the article and check your predictions.

4 Read the text again and answer these questions.

1. Why were there no brakes on the plane?
2. Why was 13th July a special day?
3. How did Anne find life difficult after her marriage to Lindbergh?
4. What did their servants do to upset the Lindberghs?
5. What happened to the Lindbergh's son?
6. Why didn't the Lindberghs stay in America after the trial?

5 Work with a partner and discuss these questions.

1. Should famous people marry shy people?
2. Is there anything Lindbergh could have done to protect his wife?

From fame to despair

On 20th May 1927 a small single-engined aeroplane loaded with 450 gallons of fuel struggled to get **airborne** as it bounced down the **runway** at Roosevelt Field, New York. To avoid extra weight, the parachute, the radio and even the brakes had been removed. At last it lifted off, just avoiding some telephone wires, and disappeared into the distance.

Thirty hours later a hundred thousand Parisians lined up at the Le Bourget Airport to wait for the arrival of the plane. It was 10 o'clock at night. Burning lanterns marked out the runway. Then came the low-pitched sound of an engine and a wave of excitement swept through the crowd. The *Spirit of St. Louis* touched down and rolled to the end of the runway. Out of the plane stepped a tall handsome American – Charles Lindbergh. He'd just become the first person to fly solo across the Atlantic, and he was destined to become one of the most famous men in the world.

He immediately set off on a tour of Europe to celebrate his **achievement**. Wherever he went he attracted crowds of people. After meeting the kings of Britain and Belgium he returned to America where, on 13th July, he was given the biggest ticker tape reception ever seen in New York. For Lindbergh it was the start of a new life of fame, adoration and money. It was, however, to be a life fraught with problems.

Two years later Lindbergh married Anne Morrow. Shy and introspective, she found it difficult suddenly being the centre of attention. They couldn't walk down the road together, go shopping or eat in a restaurant without photographers or journalists following them.

The birth of their son Charles in 1930 gave them great joy. But the interest of the public only increased and journalists did everything they could to get information about them, including bribing their servants. One night in 1932, while the Lindberghs were chatting in another room, their son was **kidnapped** from his cot. A ransom note was found asking for $50,000. The Lindberghs paid the money but their son was not returned. Ten weeks later his body was found in some nearby woods. Two years later a man was arrested and charged with his murder. The Lindberghs were then forced to endure a six-week **trial** in the media spotlight.

After the trial they fled to Britain to try and lead a normal life. They needed to **escape** the media attention and recover from the trauma of losing their child.

LANGUAGE STUDY

Sequencing events

1 Look at these sentences and answer the questions.

a ***After*** *meeting the kings of Britain and Belgium he returned to America by boat.*
b ***After*** *he met the kings of Britain and Belgium he returned to America by boat.*
c ***Before*** *he returned to America by boat he met the kings of Britain and Belgium.*
d ***After*** *the trial they fled to Britain.*

1 Do the first three sentences have similar or different meanings?
2 In which sentences are *after* / *before* followed by:
- the past simple?
- the *-ing* form?
- a noun?

2 Complete this sentence.

We can use *before* and *after* to talk about a sequence of events. They can be followed by ____________, ____________ or ____________.

3 Look at these two pairs of sentences. What's the difference between *after* and *afterwards*, and *before* and *beforehand*?

1 ***After*** *arriving in Paris Lindbergh set off on a tour of Europe.*
Lindbergh arrived in Paris, and ***afterwards*** *he set off on a tour of Europe.*
2 *Lindbergh became famous* ***before*** *he married Anne Morrow.*
Lindbergh married Anne Morrow. He had become famous ***beforehand****.*

4 Look at these sentences and complete the rule.

While *the Lindberghs were chatting in another room their son was kidnapped.*
Two years ***later*** *a man was arrested.*
Their son had been kidnapped two years ***earlier****.*

We can use ____________ to talk about two events that are happening at the same time. We can use ____________ and ____________ to talk about the different times that two events happen.

5 Compare the meanings of *afterwards* / *beforehand* with *later* / *earlier*. Which words mean:

a after / before that time? b after / before that event?

Grammar reference page 26

6 Choose the correct alternatives.

Lindbergh in shock new family claim

(1) *After / before* conducting DNA tests, Munich scientists have revealed that Charles Lindbergh had a secret second family in Germany (2) *before / while* he was apparently happily married to Anne Morrow. Even (3) *later / before* the scientists made their announcement, the three children of this family, who only discovered their father's true identity (4) *after / afterwards* his death in 1974, were sure they knew who their father was. They say that he met their mother, Brigitte Hesshaimer, 17 years (5) *earlier / before* in 1957. According to one newspaper, some time (6) *afterwards / later* Lindbergh met Brigitte's sister and also had two sons with her, but this has not been proved.

The announcement about Lindbergh's second family attracted a lot of media attention. (7) *Afterwards / After* Lindbergh's American and German children said that they intend to meet regularly and may become close, but the gap of so many years cannot be bridged in a few hours.

7 Work with a partner. Should we admire Lindbergh, sympathise with him or condemn him? Discuss your ideas.

What's your verdict?

Speaking **1** Are famous people and their family and friends entitled to privacy, or is it acceptable for the media to publish what it wants about them? Look at these situations and decide what your opinion is.

1 A famous fashion model, Kate Warner, makes a lot of extra money by inviting photographers into her home to take pictures of herself with her new baby. These photos are published in a popular celebrity magazine. One day she is secretly photographed while working out in a private gym. Three days later the photos are published in another magazine without the model's permission. The model decides to sue the magazine for publishing photos that invade her private life.

Your verdict: should the magazine have to pay compensation to the model?

2 A famous sports star, Tom Banks, has been charged by the police for injuring a man when he was involved in a fight in a pub. The man is now in hospital. Banks claims he was nowhere near the scene of the crime. He is allowed to remain free until the trial. Forty journalists and photographers wait outside the front and back doors of his house. They are trying to photograph and speak to the star. The sports star phones the police complaining he can't go outside the door of his own house and his family are getting very upset.

Your verdict: should the police have the power to move the journalists away?

3 A journalist manages to plant a listening device in the hotel room of a famous politician, John Daniels, who has always promoted family values. The next day the intimate conversation between the politician and a woman (who is not his wife) is printed in a newspaper.

Your verdict: should the politician be able to sue the newspaper?

4 Milly Kaye lives next to Jamie Lewis, who is a famous pop star in a boy band. The newspapers keep phoning her up late at night to try and get information about his new girlfriend, Sam, who presents a pop TV programme for teenagers. A team of photographers are outside her house every night and she can't sleep because of the noise and TV lights. There's nowhere to park her car at night, either. Milly usually enjoys reading the newspapers and watching stories about celebrities on TV, but she has never experienced this behaviour by journalists and photographers before. One day she comes out of the house and loses her temper with them. She damages their cars and breaks several expensive cameras.

Your verdict: should the newspapers be able to sue Milly for the damage she did?

2 Work in groups and discuss your opinions. Can your group reach an agreement?

3 What rules could be introduced to protect the privacy of famous people? Think about photographs, articles in the newspapers, their homes, and their friends and families.

CD-ROM For more activities go to **Lifestyle Unit 2**

3 A place to live

LEARNING AIMS

- Can modify comparisons
- Can describe houses
- Can use vocabulary for renting accommodation

Lead-in

1 Match the words in the box to the correct picture.

bungalow	cottage	flat	semi-detached house	terraced house

2 Work with a partner. Talk about your house. Use these questions to help you.

- Where is it?
- What does it look like?
- How many rooms does it have?
- Is it typical of houses in your country?
- What do you like and dislike about it?

Reading

1 Match these words to the photos in the magazine extract on page 11.

narrow boat	warehouse	windmill

2 Before the three places became homes, what do you think they were used for?

3 **06** Work in groups of three. Each person reads about **one** of the unusual homes on page 11 and writes notes in the appropriate column of the table.

	Warehouse	**Windmill**	**Narrow boat**
Location		ESSEX, IN THE COUNTRY	
Age			
Number of bedrooms			
Living room			
Kitchen	Stainless steel and natural wood, futuristic		
Bathrooms			
Main advantages			Nice way of life, friendly people
Main disadvantage			

4 Take it in turns to talk about the unusual homes in the magazine extract. Complete the other columns in the table with the relevant information.

5 In your group discuss which of the homes you would prefer to live in and why.

a

b

c

SOMEWHERE *completely different*

1

I live in London in a warehouse flat. I love it. It's got much more character than most modern flats. It's on the top floor of a converted 19th century tea warehouse, and it's basically one large room with very high white walls and an enormous wooden floor. The living room area is really light and spacious. There's only one bedroom, which is on a balcony above the living area. Leading off this is a fantastic bathroom which is really luxurious. The kitchen's under the balcony. It's very futuristic – all stainless steel and natural wood. I really love the huge windows which look onto the River Thames. It's a wonderful location to live in too, within easy walking distance of restaurants, bars, shops, and the tube. The only problem is it's very expensive to live here and I have to work hard to pay for it.

2

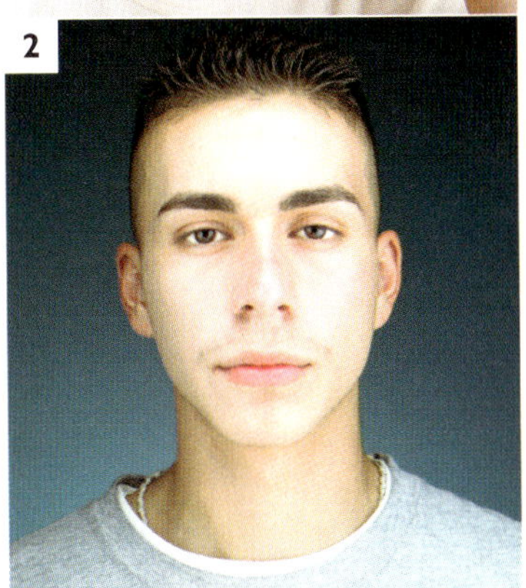

I live in Essex with my parents, my sister, and our two dogs in a windmill! It's really old, late 18th century, I think. We moved here because my parents wanted to leave London and live in the country. The great thing about it is that all the rooms are round, which makes it seem really different from most other houses, and the ceilings are quite low, which makes it cosy. Of course, we get lots of exercise going up and down stairs all the time. The kitchen is on the first floor. It's old-fashioned but we like it and we spend most of our time there. The living room is on the second floor. It's got old photographs of the windmill on the walls. There are four bedrooms on the top two floors – mine's on the top floor – and three bathrooms. We've got a lovely large garden. It's a nice house but it's a long way from town, so I always need a lift when I go out.

3

My house is a narrow boat, moored just outside Leeds. It's 25 years old and about 20 metres long and two metres wide, so all the rooms are much smaller than a normal house. It's fine for me though. I bought the boat after leaving university because I couldn't afford a house. Inside there's a very cosy living room and a well-equipped kitchen area. There are also two small bedrooms and a shower room. In summer, if I want to sit outside, there's space for a table and chairs on the open deck. The engine does a maximum of 10 km/hour. Travelling along the canal really suits me. I think that people who live on the water are friendlier. But the maintenance costs are quite high, with servicing the engine and repainting the boat every year.

6 Work with a partner and discuss these questions.

1. Do you know of any other unusual homes?
2. What would your ideal home look like? Think about the size, the style of architecture, the furniture and décor.

LANGUAGE STUDY

Modifying comparisons

1 Are these statements about the unusual homes true or false?

1 The warehouse is larger than the narrow boat. ☐

2 The windmill is as modern inside as the warehouse. ☐

3 The windmill is more convenient for the shops than the warehouse. ☐

4 The narrow boat is the least spacious. ☐

5 The warehouse has the fewest rooms. ☐

2 Which words in the sentences in Ex 1:

1 compare two things which are different?
2 compare two things which are similar?
3 compare one thing which is different from the others in a group?

3 You can make comparative and superlative adjectives stronger and weaker by using modifiers. Look at these example sentences and complete the table.

*The inside of the windmill is **nowhere near** as modern as the warehouse, but it's **nearly** as high as the warehouse.*

*The narrow boat is **far** cheaper than the warehouse, but it's **much** smaller.*
*The warehouse flat is **by far** the most luxurious.*
*The warehouse is **a bit** older than the narrow boat.*
*The warehouse is **much** more convenient for shopping than the windmill.*
*The narrow boat is **not quite** as unusual as the windmill.*

	Comparative	*as ... as*	Superlative
Strong		nowhere near	
Weak			

Grammar reference page 27

4 Work with a partner. Make true sentences using these phrases.

Examples:
nearly as long as: *Luke's hair is nearly as long as his sister's.*
by far the most difficult: *Last year's exam was by far the most difficult I've ever done.*

1 much more important than …
2 nearly as dangerous as …
3 by far the least enjoyable …
4 far less difficult than …
5 nowhere near as tiring as …
6 much further than …
7 by far the fewest …
8 a bit more interesting than …
9 by far the best …
10 by far the most expensive …

5 Work with a partner. Choose **one** of the following pairs of items. How many ways can you compare them?

- Two countries you both know
- Two people you both know
- Two buildings you both know
- Two celebrities you both know
- Two interests or hobbies you both know
- Two different types of food you both know

Flat to let

Vocabulary and listening

1 Work in a small group. Discuss the answers to these questions. Use a dictionary if necessary.

1. Who rents a flat, a landlord / landlady or a tenant?
2. Who lets a flat a landlord / landlady or a tenant?
3. Would you share a flat if you had the choice? Why? / Why not?
4. Do you need to buy a bed, table and chairs for a flat which is furnished?
5. Would someone who is very clean be happy to move into an immaculate flat?
6. How often do you normally have to pay rent?
7. If you move into a fully-equipped flat, what kinds of things would you expect to find in it?
8. How does a flat's location affect its price?
9. If a flat was available from 24th November, why couldn't you move in on 23rd November?
10. If the price was £400 inclusive, how much would you have to pay for the gas and electricity bills?

2 Read the introduction about Maria. What kind of place do you think she is looking for?

Maria, who is Brazilian, has just arrived in Edinburgh. She's going to do some postgraduate research at Edinburgh University. She's staying with a Scottish friend, Fiona, until she can find a place of her own. She's busy flat hunting.

3 **07** Listen to the first part of Maria's conversation with Fiona about some advertisements that she's found. Which of these are important to Maria?

1 How much it costs ☐ 2 If there's parking ☐ 3 Where it's located ☐
4 The size ☐ 5 If it's well-decorated ☐

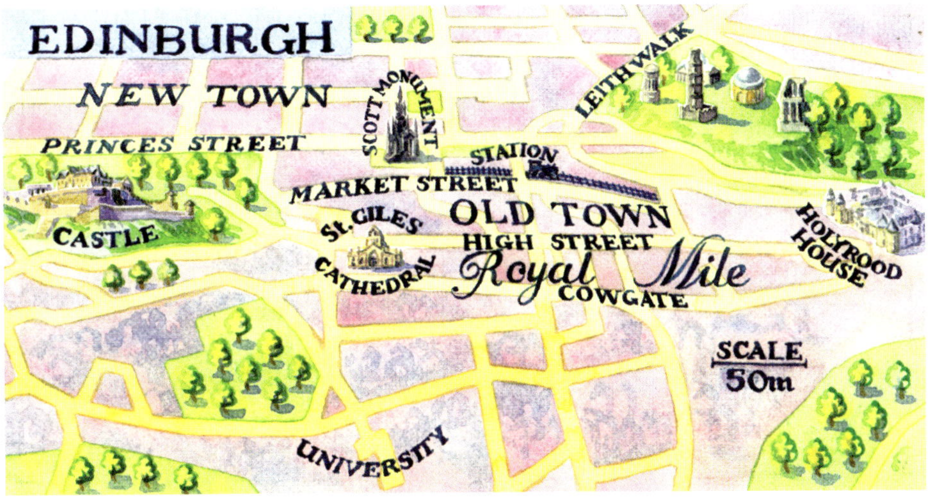

4 **08** Listen to the second part of the conversation. What's wrong with the flats in each of these locations and which one does she finally choose to go and look at?

1 Old Town: ____________ 3 Off Princes Street: ____________
2 New Town: ____________ 4 Leith Walk: ____________

5 Listen again. Imagine you are going to spend some time studying in Edinburgh and you need a flat. Which one would you choose? Why?

Speaking

1 Work with a partner. You are going to have a telephone conversation to discuss suitable accommodation for four people who are coming to Edinburgh to study at the Castle School of English. Your aim is to find accommodation for each one. Student A turn to page 29. Student B turn to page 32.

CD-ROM For more activities go to **Lifestyle Unit 3**

4 Life changes

LEARNING AIMS

- Can use verbs for talking about the future
- Can conduct a class survey
- Can use phrasal verbs for life changes

Lead-in

1 Look at the table and read the examples of things you are allowed to do in Britain at different ages. How are British laws different from the laws in your country?

At 16 you can ...
- leave school
- get married with parental consent
- work full time
- buy cigarettes
- ride a moped

At 17 you can ...
- drive a car
- ride a small motorbike
- be sent to prison

At 18 you can ...
- get married without parental consent
- get a tattoo without parental consent
- buy an alcoholic drink in a pub
- buy a house
- vote

Reading

1 You are going to read about four 18-year-olds talking about being 18. What things do you think they'll talk about?

2 **09** Read the texts from a magazine. Who:

1 won't be able to see his girlfriend?
2 hopes to go to higher education next year?
3 is concerned about more than a career?
4 is worried about not getting a good job?
5 wants to live in New York?
6 would like to help other people?
7 feels ready to become an adult?
8 knows what he / she is going to study?

1

This is my last year at school and it feels a bit odd. I'm ready to leave, but I'll miss my girlfriend. I definitely expect to have a good time at university. I think I'll be happy wherever I go. It's college – there'll be people there and they'll be cool. I'm not worried about growing up and becoming an adult. It's cool. *Peter, USA*

2

I think the most important thing is to get a career. Lots of people end up getting badly paid jobs. I don't want to be one of them. So I'm going to try to get a job this year and save up enough money to get to university next year. *Maria, Kenya*

3

Becoming a doctor is the only thing I've ever really considered doing in life. So I intend to study medicine at university. I like the idea of helping and meeting different people. I'll probably get married and be a father one day, but it will happen when it happens. *James, Wales*

4

Right now I'm training to be a contemporary dancer and my ambitions are to get into a well-known company and to live in New York. I'm going to go there as soon as I complete my studies. I want to succeed at all levels – my work, my professional and my emotional life. *Sophie, France*

3 Work with a partner. Read the texts again and discuss these questions.

1 Which two people have the clearest ideas about what they intend to do with their lives?
2 Who do you think will be the most successful? The happiest? The most disappointed? Why?
3 What do you think each of the people will be doing in ten years' time?

Listening **1** 10 Listen to Peter, Maria, James and Sophie. They are now 28 and they are talking about how their lives have changed since they were 18. Complete the first column of the table with notes on what their jobs are now.

	Now	Future
Peter		
Maria		
James		
Sophie		

2 Listen again and complete the second column of the table with their plans for the future.

3 Work with a partner. Discuss the ways that Peter, Maria, James and Sophie's lives are different from the predictions they made when they were 18.

Example:
When Peter was 18 he was very confident about the future. He's far less confident about the future now.

Phrasal verbs: life changes

Vocabulary **1** Read these sentences and match the phrasal verbs to the definitions.

1 I'm not worried about **growing up** and becoming an adult.
2 Lots of people **end up** getting badly paid jobs.
3 My ambitions are to **get into** a well-known company.
4 I'm going to **set up** my own business.
5 I had to **move on** and do something with my life.
6 I **took** a year **off** and worked as a volunteer.
7 I **looked around** for something else.

a begin something different
b start something
c have time away from something
d arrive at a particular place or state
e changing from being a child to an adult
f be allowed to join
g try to find something you want or need

2 Work with a partner and discuss these questions.

1 Have you ever taken any time off for any reason?
2 What was the most enjoyable and the most difficult thing for you about growing up?
3 What do you think the hardest thing is about setting up a new business?
4 What do you hope you'll end up doing in your life?

LANGUAGE STUDY

Verbs for talking about the future

1 Read these sentences and answer the questions.

a *I **hope** that I'll be rich and successful.*
b *He **intends** to get married next year.*
c *I'm **due** to start a new job next week.*
d *She'**d like** to look around and get a better job.*
e *He **expects** to get into university.*
f *We're **hoping** to start our own company.*
g *We're **aiming** to save hard and buy a new car.*
h *I **expect** that he'll work abroad again this summer.*

1 In which of these sentences is the speaker:
 a more sure that something will happen?
 b less sure that something will happen?
2 In which sentences is the first verb followed by *to* + infinitive?
3 Which verbs can be followed by (*that*) + verb?

Grammar reference page 27

2 Complete these lists of verbs from Ex 1 to talk about the future.

More sure: *intend* ________________________________
less sure: *hope* ________________________________

3 Choose the correct alternative.

1 Rachel's decided to decorate her room. She *intends / hopes* to paint the walls lilac.
2 Today I *aim / expect* to finish writing an economics essay, but I'm not sure I'll get it all done.
3 I *expect / would like* to start a family when I'm in my late twenties. I love children.
4 Carl's so popular these days that I *expect / hope* he won't have much time to see me.

4 Work with a partner. Discuss these questions.

1 What are you hoping to do in the next few months?
2 What do you expect to achieve in this course?
3 When are you due to come to your next lesson?

Jobs and courses

Vocabulary and pronunciation

1 Complete the list of jobs and courses. Compare your answers with other students.

1 Doctor: *Medicine*
2 Accountant: __________
3 Historian: __________
4 Linguist: __________
5 __________: Pharmacy
6 __________: Psychology
7 __________: Physics
8 __________: Physiotherapy
9 Solicitor: __________
10 __________: Statistics
11 Teacher: __________

2 11 Listen and match each word from Ex 1 to the correct stress pattern.

O	Oo	Ooo	oOo	oOoo	ooOo	oooOoo
	Doctor				*Statistician*	*Physiotherapist*
	Medicine					*Physiotherapy*

3 Listen again and repeat the words.

4 Work with a partner and discuss these questions.

1 Do you do any of the jobs in Ex 1? Which one is the best paid in your country?
2 Which of the jobs in Ex 1 do you think you'd be good at / dreadful at?
3 Which of the courses would interest you, or bore you? Why?

A letter to me

Writing 1 Imagine yourself at the beginning of your career. Write a letter to yourself which you will read in 30 years time. Say what you are doing now and what you hope to do in the future. Use the example to help you.

> Dear Me,
>
> When I read this letter again in 30 years time, I'll be 50 years old. That's hard to imagine at the moment. Right now I'm in my second year at university. I'm studying journalism. I hope to graduate with a good degree, but I know that this is a very competitive profession and any practical experience I can get by actually working for a newspaper will be more important than my qualification. So I'm hoping to spend my holidays working for the local paper. It's not very glamorous, but I expect to make lots of useful contacts.
>
> I'm aiming to join a national newspaper within five years of graduating, or else I'll give it up as I don't intend to spend my entire life writing about local events.
>
> I'd like to be working in television or even radio by the time I'm 35. After that who knows ...

Speaking 1 Complete the questionnaire and compare your answers with other students.

HOW INDEPENDENT ARE YOU?

1 **When you need to buy clothes for a special occasion, who helps you choose?**
- a Someone in my family. They know what suits me.
- b My friends. They know what's fashionable.
- c I go by myself. I know exactly what I want to wear.

2 **Who would you go to first if you argue with a boyfriend / girlfriend?**
- a Someone in my family.
- b My friends, and we'd gossip about it.
- c I'd sort it out myself.

3 **When you have to make decisions about your course or career, who do you ask for advice?**
- a My family.
- b My friends.
- c I make the decision by myself.

4 **When you go on holiday, who do you prefer to go with?**
- a My family.
- b My friends.
- c I go on my own. It's more exciting!

5 **You're going to have a special celebration for getting an exciting new job. Who plans it?**
- a My family – they'll be paying!
- b My friends, to give me a surprise.
- c Me. I want to make sure I celebrate in the way I want.

2 Check your answers on page 32 to see how independent you are.

3 Work with a partner. You are going to prepare a questionnaire. Choose a topic and think of a title for your questionnaire, for example: *How ambitious are you? How important is marriage to you? What do you think of politics?*

4 Write your questions and prepare an answer key. Use the ideas in Ex 1 to help you.

5 Interview at least four members of your class and make a note of their answers.

6 Prepare a short talk with your partner to report your findings to the class. Start like this: *Our questionnaire was about ambition. We asked fourteen students the following questions ...*

CD-ROM For more activities go to **Lifestyle Unit 4**

5 Review

Lead-in **1** Do you watch or listen to chat shows? Which is your favourite?

Language study

1 You are going to listen to a radio programme called *Paul Logan's Chat Show*. The two guests on the show are Megan Robinson, a tennis player and Johnny Wade, a comedian and writer. Write six questions you expect the host to ask the guests.

2 12 Listen and compare Paul Logan's questions with the ones you wrote in Ex 1. How many of them are the same?

3 Listen again and answer these questions.

1 Where does Johnny get the inspiration for the characters in his new TV series?
2 When is Johnny's new series due to start?
3 What title has Megan just won?
4 How well can Johnny play tennis?
5 Does Megan train harder before or after lunch?
6 What is the hardest thing about being a tennis player for her?
7 What two things is she planning to do next?
8 How does Paul Logan feel at the end of the interview?

4 Complete these sentences from the listening with the correct form of the words in brackets. Check your answers in Listening script 12 on page 31.

1 After (listen) ______________ to them I always make notes on what they have said.
2 The reviews say it's (by far funny) ______________ new show this year.
3 It's (due start) ______________ this week.
4 I (usually train) ______________ for a couple of hours with my coach in the mornings before (do) ______________ an hour in the gym.
5 I really need to be (a bit light) ______________ than I am.
6 I intend (have) ______________ a long break.

5 Look at the pictures and complete the story. Compare your ideas with a partner.

1 Paul met Julie at a party. They danced for at least half an hour together. While they were dancing, ______________

2 After Paul got home, ______________

3 Julie washed her hair and put on her make-up. Earlier she had bought ______________

4 Julie and Paul had dinner together. Afterwards, ______________

5 Paul loves Julie very much. He intends ______________

6 Invent your own short story. Include at least four of the words in the box. Tell your story to a partner.

after	afterwards	at least	before	beforehand	by far	earlier	expect
hope	intend	later	more than	while	would like to		

Vocabulary

1 Work with a partner. Student A turn to page 29. Student B turn to page 32. Read how to play the 'Five minute challenge' and play the game.

2 Work in a group of two to four players. Read how to play the 'Word buster' game and play the game.

WORD BUSTER

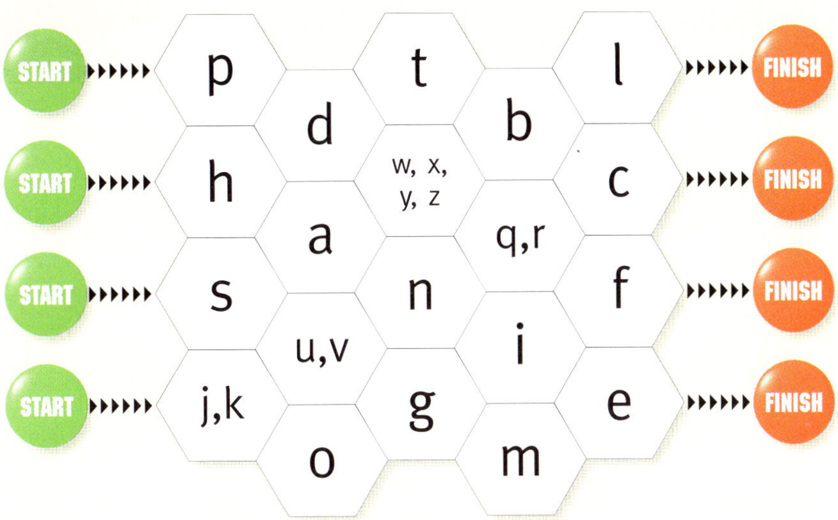

HOW TO PLAY

1 Each player puts a counter on one of the four coloured start positions. The aim is to reach the other side of the board.

2 Each player can only move one space at a time. Each player must choose the next letter he / she wants to move to before throwing the dice. For example, if a player is on 'a' he / she can move to, 'w, x, y, z' or 'n'.

3 The player throws the dice. The number on the dice (1–6) relates to one of the six categories. The player has 30 seconds to think of a word in that category beginning with the correct letter.

4 If the word is correct, the player moves on to the letter space and the next player continues. If the player cannot think of a word, he / she does not move.

5 The first player to reach the finish is the winner.

CATEGORIES

1 Types of houses and rooms. Adjectives to describe rooms

2 Jobs and courses

3 Buying and renting accommodation

4 Adverbs of frequency

5 Verbs for talking about the future

6 Phrasal verbs to describe life changes

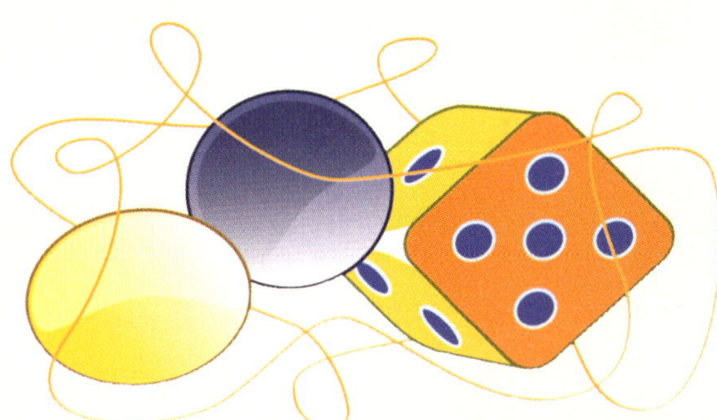

Song

1 Read the factfile about Burt Bacharach and Hal David and answer these questions.

1. What are they famous for?
2. When did they first work together?
3. How many hits in the top 40 have they had?
4. How many different versions of *I say a little prayer for you* are there?

factfile

Frank Sinatra, Whitney Houston, Barbra Streisand, Dionne Warwick and Aretha Franklin are just some of the stars who have sung songs that have been written by Burt Bacharach and Hal David. Their collaboration goes back to 1958, and, even before that, Bacharach was Marlene Dietrich's musical director. During their long careers as songwriters they've written over fifty top forty hits such as *What the world needs now, Do you know the way to San José?*, and *Raindrops keep falling on my head* – which featured in the 2004 film *Spiderman 2*, but which they originally wrote for Paul Newman and Robert Redford in the Oscar winning *Butch Cassidy and the Sundance Kid*. There are at least five versions of *I say a little prayer for you*. Usually it's just the pop stars who become famous, but Burt Bacharach and Hal David have written some of the world's best known songs.

2 13 Listen to the song. Which word or words in the box best describe how the woman feels?

cheerful	confident	desperate	disappointed	hopeful	lonely
miserable	strong				

I say a little prayer for you

The moment I wake up
Before I put on my make-up
I say a little prayer for you
While combing my hair now
And wondering what dress to wear now
I say a little prayer for you

Chorus

Forever, forever, you'll stay in my heart
And I will love you
Forever, forever, we never will part
Oh how I'll love you
Together, together
That's how it must be
To live without you
Would only be heartbreak for me

I run for the bus dear
While riding I think of us dear
I say a little prayer for you
At work I just take time
And all through my coffee break time
I say a little prayer for you

Chorus x 2

My darling, believe me
For me there is no one, but you
Please love me true, 'cause I'm in love with you
Answer my prayer, say you'll love me true

Chorus

3 Are these statements about the woman's life true or false? Underline the words in the song which support your answers.

1. She puts on make-up as soon as she wakes up. ☐
2. She usually wears a dress. ☐
3. She would be sad if the man left her. ☐
4. She goes to work by bus. ☐
5. She is very busy at work. ☐
6. She has other men in her life. ☐

4 What advice would you give the woman in the song?

Speaking: a chat show interview

1 Work in groups of three. You are going to create a chat show interview. Follow the instructions.

Step 1: Prepare the information you need

- In your group choose two celebrities and a host to introduce the show and interview the celebrity guests.
- Make up a life story and some interesting facts about each of the celebrity guests by completing the *Celebrity guest role card*. Then think of questions for the hosts to ask by completing the *Host's question card*.

Celebrity GUEST ROLE CARD

★ Job *(For example: film actor, pop star)*
____

★ Name (*Think of a good celebrity-style name*)
____

★ Age ____________________

★ Where you come from ____________________

★ Why you are famous
____

★ When and how you started your career
____

★ Your family life
____

★ What you are doing at the moment
____
____

★ Your future plans
____
____

★ A recent piece of good or bad news *(For example: you are going to make a new film or your marriage just ended)*
____
____

Host QUESTION CARD

★ How are you going to introduce the show? *(For example: Hello and welcome to the Marta and Sohei Evening Show!)* ____________________
____

★ How are you going to introduce each guest?
____

★ Make a list of four questions to ask each of the guests. *(Don't ask each guest the same questions)*
____________________?
____________________?
____________________?
____________________?

★ What are you going to ask each guest about his / her recent good or bad news? *(For example: Is it true what the newspapers are saying that your marriage is ending?)*
____________________?
____________________?
____________________?
____________________?

★ How are you going to finish the show?
____
____
____

Step 2: Practise your show Practise your show once or twice. It should last for five to ten minutes.

Step 3: Perform the show When each group performs their chat show the rest of the class is the audience. The audience should clap and cheer at the start of the show and when each guest is introduced. The audience should also ask questions at the end of the show.

Extra practice

Unit 1

1 Rearrange these words to make correct sentences. Sometimes there is more than one possible answer.

Example:
London to day often we for the go
We often go to London for the day.

1 go never Monday out we evenings on

____

____

2 July holiday in usually on go I

____

____

3 read I on newspaper in Sundays bed always a

____

____

4 often during to music he lessons his listens

____

____

5 go in camping sometimes spring they

____

____

2 In which sentences in Ex 1 can you put the adverb of frequency at the beginning or the end of the sentence? ________

3 Complete the dialogue. What's Jo's problem?

____

Pete: What time / get up / in the morning?
What time do you get up in the morning?

Jo: Usually at about 7.00, sometimes 7.30.

Pete: What time / leave home?
(1) ______________________________

Jo: Well, I have to leave at about 8.15 if I want to avoid the morning traffic.

Pete: How / get / to work?
(2) ______________________________

Jo: I used to go by car but now I go by bike. I need the exercise!

Pete: How often do you arrive at work after 9.15?

Jo: About / twice / week.
(3) ______________________________

Pete: Mm. What / your boss / think / about it?
(4) ______________________________

Jo: She / want me / arrive at 9.00 / every day.
(5) ______________________________

Pete: I'm not surprised! What / do?
(6) ______________________________

Jo: I'm a teacher.

Pete: You're joking!

4 Read the text. Which job is described? ____________

lawyer	policeman	pilot	travel agent

I usually work for about eight hours a day but sometimes I work for longer. I wear a uniform and every day I work with different people. I earn quite a lot of money as I have a responsible job. I have to stay fit, and I have a health check at least twice a year. Some people think that with modern technology there isn't much for us to do, but I have to get trained on the new equipment about once a month, and if there's an emergency then we have to leap into action. I enjoy going to all the different places although we almost always have to turn straight round and come back again. Occasionally there's some sort of delay, which means we stay overnight, but that happens less than three or four times a year. Next year I'm going to further destinations so that might make it more interesting.

5 Read the text again and find:

1 four more time phrases (example: *about eight hours a day*)

____

2 four adverbs of frequency

____

6 Write a description of one of the other jobs in Ex 4. Use at least three time phrases and three adverbs of frequency.

____

____

____

____

____

____

Unit 2

1 Rearrange these letters to find six different ways that people have become famous.

Example: starit = *artist*

1 omscpore ______________________

2 tlaleb crneda ______________________

3 corat ______________________

4 albtoloefr ______________________

5 sniten alyrep ______________________

6 rteodirc ______________________

2 Complete the table with the words in the box. Then underline the stressed syllable in each word.

actress awful borrow complain decent delicate fantastic photography psychologist strategy terrific whisper

Number of syllables

2	3	4
actress		

3 Which word in the table with two syllables doesn't follow the normal rule for word stress?

4 Replace the underlined words with the words in the box.

compensation escape kidnapped sue trial verdict

1 They said on the news that he had been taken prisoner.

2 It is the biggest court case in Hollywood.

3 He tried to make a legal claim against the newspaper.

4 She wanted payment of £20,000 for her injuries.

5 The jury took 2 days to reach a decision.

6 We couldn't wait to get away from the classroom.

5 Complete the story with the words in the box.

afterwards earlier (x2) later leaving parking while

Revenge is forever

Before (1) ______________ his office Cliff Drysdale took out his gun from the drawer in his desk. Ten minutes (2) ______________ he was in his car heading towards the town centre. He listened to the radio (3) ______________ he was driving. He heard the news that he was expecting. Several hours (4) ______________ Shaw had broken out of Strangeways Top Security Prison and he was now on the run. Drysdale feared that Shaw was heading towards the home of Judge Adams. Drysdale parked his car in Long Road. After (5) ______________ he walked into Cherry Tree Road where the judge lived. He had phoned the judge half an hour (6) ______________ but there had been no reply. He had phoned the police immediately (7)______________. They had promised to go over and check the house; so why weren't they there now?

6 Imagine it is now three hours after Drysdale arrived at the judge's house. Write the next chapter in the story. Use at least four linking words that sequence the events.

Unit 3

1 Look at these advertisements for accommodation to rent in Cambridge. Match the people to the accommodation.

1 Harry and Jenna's family like eating outdoors. ____

2 Matt wants to share a house but doesn't have time to do any housework. ____

3 Paula wants to share a house but wants her own bathroom and doesn't like animals. ____

4 Ian and Ruth are married. They don't have a car and often commute to work by train. ____

a Room in shared country cottage, off-road parking, f/f. £250 pcm. Tel 01223 34895

b Two bedroom flat. Spacious, f/f, fitted kitchen, c/h, nr railway station. £700 pcm. Tel 01223 29475

c Single furnished room with own shower in family semi-detached house outskirts of city. £250 pcm. inc. Tel 01223 78345

d Room in large luxury country house, 10 miles city centre, u/f, suit n/s professional person. £400 pcm. Tel 01456 78393

e Double room to let in large city centre house, immaculate decoration, en suite, u/f, n/s, no pets. Suit professional. Tel 01223 47883

f 3 bedroom f/f house with parking. Quiet road. Large kitchen. Garden with barbecue area. £750 pcm inc. Tel 01223 37623

g Room for n/s in shared f/f c/h house with cleaner. 2 miles from city centre. Suit postgraduate or professional. Tel 01223 37283

2 Find abbreviations in the advertisements in Ex 1 which mean:

1 each room is fully furnished ______

2 it is unfurnished ______

3 there's central heating ______

4 per month ______

5 it is situated near to ______

6 we do not want someone who smokes ______

7 the price is inclusive of all bills ______

3 Complete the sentences using the information in the table. Use the words in brackets and one of these modifiers: *a bit, far, much, not quite.*

	Australia	**UK**
Area	7,682,300 km^2	241,752km^2
Population	20,240,000	58,395,000
Rainfall per year	455 mm	1,151 mm
Average length of life	80.0 years	78.3 years
Income per person/year	US$ 24,000	US$ 31,150

1 The area of Australia is (big) ____________ than the area of UK.

2 The population of the UK is (great) ____________ than the population of Australia.

3 The UK is (wet) ____________ than Australia.

4 The lives of people in Australia are (long) ____________ than the lives of people in the UK.

5 People in Australia are (rich) ____________ as people in the UK.

4 Make sentences comparing your country with the UK. If you are not sure of the information about your country, guess.

1 Area: ______________________________

____

2 Population: ______________________________

____

3 Rainfall: ______________________________

____

4 Average length of life: ______________________________

____

5 Income per person: ______________________________

____

Unit 4

1 Complete the puzzle with names of jobs. What's the extra job? ________

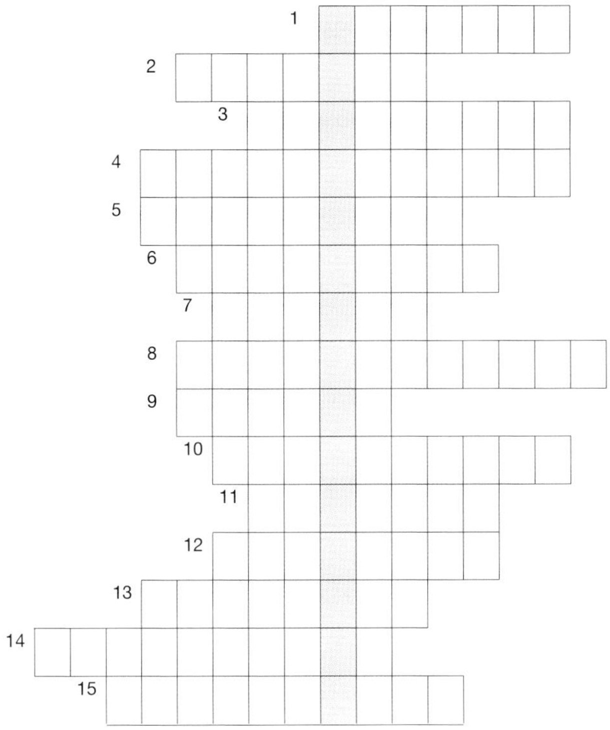

Clues

1 I decorate your house. I'm a ____.
2 You meet this person in your English classes.
3 I'm a scientist. I work with heat and light. I'm a ____.
4 I work with facts and figures. I'm a ____.
5 If you're in trouble with the law, you need my help.
6 I study the past. I'm a ____.
7 You see this person when you're ill.
8 I study people's minds and their behaviour. I'm a ____.
9 I entertain people. I love ballet. I'm a ____.
10 I give people their medicine. I'm a ____.
11 I can help people who want to get fit. I'm a ____.
12 You can hear my music in a concert hall. I'm a ____.
13 I speak several languages. I'm a ____.
14 I report the news. I'm a ____.
15 I count cash, and write reports about money. I'm an ____.

2 Rearrange the words to make questions about the future.

Example:
do / are / life / to / hoping / what / with / you / your ?
What are you hoping to do with your life?

1 course / what / intend / after / do / this / do / finish / you / you / to?
____
____

2 is / due / class / next / start / to / when / your?
____
____

3 do / future / in / like / the / to / what / would / you ?
____
____

4 do / get / married / to / soon / you / expect ?
____
____

5 do / holiday / hope / next / spend / 'll / where / you / your / you ?
____
____

3 Answer the questions in Ex 2 with true statements about yourself.

1 ____
____
2 ____
____
3 ____
____
4 ____
____
5 ____
____

4 Complete these sentences with the correct form of the phrasal verbs in the box.

end up	get into	grow up	look around
move on	set up	take off	

1 I ______________ in a small village in the middle of the countryside.
2 It's easy to ______________ in a job you don't really enjoy.
3 I'm planning to ______________ an internet company with my friend Matt.
4 I would like to ______________ a famous law firm when I graduate.
5 I'm ______________ for a job in education at the moment.
6 I've decided to ______________ a year ______________ before going to university.
7 I do the same thing every day. I need to ______________ and find a better job.

Grammar reference

Unit 1

Present simple

Form

I	play	football
You		
We		
They		
He	plays	football
She		
It		

Statement: *He goes to bed late.*
Negative statement: *They don't get up until 12 o'clock.*
Question: *Do you study chess games?*

Use

The present simple is sometimes described as the 'normal' tense to talk about the present, when there's no particular reason for using one of the other tenses. You use it to talk about:

- time in general: *She works for an oil company in Japan.*
- routines and habits: *I always get up late on Sundays.*
- things that are always true: *It isn't very warm in winter.*
- likes, dislikes and interests: *He doesn't like cheese.*

Adverbs of frequency

You use adverbs of frequency to say how often you do something. The most common ones are:
never, seldom, rarely, occasionally, sometimes, frequently, often, usually, normally, always

Adverbs of frequency usually appear between the subject and the verb:
*We **usually** eat out on Friday evenings.*
*I **sometimes** forget to lock my car.*

With the verb *be* the adverb of frequency appears after the verb.
***I am sometimes** late for my classes.*

Occasionally, sometimes, frequently, often, usually and *normally* can also appear at the beginning or end of sentences. When they appear at the beginning of a sentence it is because we want to emphasise the frequency:

***Occasionally** she works until eight o'clock in the evening.*
*She works until eight o'clock in the evening **occasionally**.*

Never, seldom, rarely and *always* are not normally used at the beginning or end of sentences.

Unit 2

Sequencing events

You can use *before, after, afterwards, beforehand, later, earlier,* and *while* to talk about the sequence of time and events.

before and *after*

Before and *after* can be followed by a noun, a verb or an *-ing* form. You use *before* and *after* to talk about the sequence of events.

***Before the concert** he talked to the musicians.*
***After** he **met** his new boss he decided to change his job.*
***Before leaving home** she wrote a letter to her parents.*

beforehand and *afterwards*

You use *beforehand* and *afterwards* to avoid repeating the noun.

*She had an appointment with her solicitor. She had seen her bank manager **beforehand**.*
= She had an appointment with her solicitor. She had seen her bank manager before the appointment with her solicitor.

*They watched the film and **afterwards** they had a meal.*
= They watched the film and after watching the film they had a meal.

while

You use *while* to talk about two events that are happening at the same time. You can use it to talk about past, present or future events.

***While** you're having your driving test tomorrow, I'll be on my way to France.*

*A burglar broke in **while** I was out shopping.*

earlier and *later*

Earlier and *later* mean 'before / after that time'.
*We arrived home at six o'clock and **later** we went out to see some friends.* (*Later* = a time after six o'clock.)

*They went to see a film in the afternoon. **Earlier** they'd had lunch together.* (*Earlier* = before the time the film began.)

You use *earlier* and *later* to talk about sequences of time. This contrasts with *before / beforehand* and *after / afterwards*, which you use to talk about sequences of events.

Unit 3

Modifying comparisons

You can compare things in several ways:

1 You can compare two things which are different using the comparative forms of adjectives:
Although my house is ***smaller*** *and* ***less spacious*** *than Anna's house, it's* ***more beautiful****.*

2 You can compare two things which are similar using *as … as*:
The kitchen is ***as large as*** *the lounge.*

You can also use ***as*** … ***as*** in negative comparisons:
The warehouse flat ***isn't as cosy as*** *the windmill.*

3 You can compare one thing which is different from the others in a group using the superlative form of adjectives.

This is the ***cheapest*** *flat but it isn't in the* ***best*** *location.*

They wanted to rent the ***most convenient*** *flat but they couldn't afford it.*

You can make comparative and superlative adjectives stronger and weaker by using modifiers.

	Comparative	***as … as***	**Superlative**
Strong	far much	nowhere near	by far
Weak	a bit	not quite nearly	______

The people are ***far friendlier*** *here* ***than*** *in the city.*

The balcony in our new house ***isn't quite as large as*** *the balcony in our old house.*

This is ***by far the most futuristic*** *flat we've seen.*

Unit 4

Future plans and intentions

You can use different verbs and the form *(be) due* to describe how sure you are that something will happen.

Sure or quite sure that something will happen: *(is) due, expect, intend*

Not sure that something will happen: *aim, hope, would like*

Her flight ***is due*** *to arrive in ten minutes.* (The time is written on the ticket.)

We ***intend*** *to redecorate the bathroom this weekend.* (We've already decided to do this.)

He's ***hoping*** *to finish his homework by eight o'clock.* (But he's not sure if it will take longer than this.)

I'd like *to go to university.* (But I can only go there if I pass my exams.)

All of these verbs and *(be) due* can be followed by the infinitive with *to*.

They***'re hoping to buy*** a new house next year.

Hope and *expect* can also be followed with *will*.
I ***hope*** *(that)* ***I'll*** pass my exams.

LIFESTYLE

Wordlist

*** the 2,500 most common English words, ** very common words, * fairly common words

Unit 1

accurate *adj* /ˈækjʊrət/ **
analyse *v* /ˈænəˌlaɪz/ ***
awful *adj* /ˈɔːfl/ **
borrow *v* /ˈbɒrəʊ/ **
caviar *n* /ˈkæviˌɑː/
citizen *n* /ˈsɪtɪzn/ ***
couch potato *n* /ˈkaʊtʃ pəˌteɪtəʊ/
deal with *v* /ˈdiːl ˌwɪð/
decent *adj* /ˈdiːsnt/ **
delicate *adj* /ˈdelɪkət/ **
fresh *adj* /freʃ/ ***
gossip *n* / gossip *v* /ˈgɒsɪp/
guess *v* /ges/ ***
guest *n* /gest/ ***
habits *n* /ˈhæbɪts/ ***
health farm *n* /ˈhelθ ˌfɑːm/
in a row *phrase* /ˌɪn ə ˈrəʊ/
journalist *n* /ˈdʒɜːnəlɪst/ **
luxury *adj* /ˈlʌkʃəri/ *
match *n* /mætʃ/ ***
media *n* /ˈmiːdɪə/ ***
mental *adj* /ˈmentl/ ***
miserable *adj* /ˈmɪz(ə)rəbl/ *
mobile *n* /ˈməʊˌbaɪl/ **
never mind *phrase* /nevə maɪnd/
no point *phrase* /ˌnəʊ ˈpɔɪnt/
occasionally *adv* /əˈkeɪʒn(ə)lɪ/ ***
often *adv* /ˈɒfn/ ***
opponent *n* /əˈpəʊnənt/ **
outfit *n* /aʊtfɪt/ *
overhear *v* /ˌəʊvəˈhɪə/
relatives *n* /ˈrelətɪvz/ **
relax *v* /rɪˈlæks/ ***
routine *n* /ˌruːˈtiːnz/ **
solve *v* /sɒlv/ ***
strategy *n* /ˈstrætədʒi/ ***
survive *v* /səˈvaɪv/ ***
tournament *n* /ˈtʊənəmənt/ **
unwind *v* /ʌnˈwaɪnd/
usually *adv* /ˈjuːʒʊəlɪ/ ***
whisper *v* /ˈwɪspə/ **
wonderful *adj* /ˈwʌndəfl/ ***
wòrthwhile *adj* /ˌwɜːθˈwaɪl/ **

Unit 2

achievement *n* /əˈtʃiːvmənt/ ***
advantage *n* /ədˈvɑːntɪdʒ/ ***
airborne *adj* /ˈeəˌbɔːn/
announcement *n* /əˈnaʊnsmənt/ ***
arrest *v* /əˈrest/ **
brake *n* /breɪk/ *
break up *v* /ˌbreɪk ˈʌp/
bribe *v* /braɪb/
bridge *v* /brɪdʒ/
bully *v* /ˈbʊli/ *
celebrity *n* /səˈlebrəti/ *
charge *v* /tʃɑːdʒ/ ***
claim *v* /kleɪm/ ***
compensation *n* /ˌkɒmpənˈseɪʃn/ **
complain *v* /kəmˈpleɪn/ ***
composer *n* /kəmˈpəʊzə/ **
condemn *v* /kənˈdem/ **
damage *n* / damage *v* /ˈdæmɪdʒ/ ***
despair *n* /dɪˈspeə/ *
desperate *adj* /ˈdesp(ə)rət/ **
device *n* /dɪˈvaɪs/ ***
director *n* /dəˈrektə; daɪˈrektə/ ***
disadvantage *n* /ˌdɪsədˈvɑːntɪdʒ/ **
discover *v* /dɪˈskʌvə/ ***
downsides *n* /ˈdaʊnˌsaɪdz/
drive to succeed *phrase* /ˌdraɪv tə səkˈsiːd/
earlier *adv* /ˈɜːlɪə/ ***
escape *v* /ɪˈskeɪp/ **
fame *n* /feɪm/ **
family values *n* /ˌfæmlɪ ˈvæljuːz/
injure *v* /ˈɪndʒə/ **
intend *v* /ɪnˈtend/ ***
intimate *adj* /ˈɪntɪmət/
introspective *adj* /ˌɪntrəˈspektɪv/
invade *v* /ɪnˈveɪd/ *
kidnap *v* /ˈkɪdnæp/ *
live up to expectations *phrase* /ˌlɪv ʌp tuː ˌekspekˈteɪʃnz/
media spotlight *n* /ˌmiːdiə ˈspɒtlaɪt/
painter *n* /ˈpeɪntə/ **
permission *n* /pəˈmɪʃn/ **
pressure *n* /ˈpreʃə/ ***
privacy *n* /ˈprɪvəsɪ/ *
protect *v* /prəˈtekt/ ***
prove *v* /pruːv/ ***
public *v* /ˈpʌblɪk/ ***
ransom *n* /ˈræns(ə)m/
reveal *v* /rɪˈviːl/ ***
runway *n* /ˈrʌnweɪ/ *
self-esteem *n* /ˌselfəˈstiːm/ *
sue *v* /suː/ **
suffer *v* /ˈsʌfə/ ***
sympathise *v* /ˈsɪmpəˌθaɪz/
temper *n* /ˈtempə/ **
terrific *adj* /təˈrɪfɪk/ *
trauma *n* /ˈtrɔːmə/
trial *n* /ˈtraɪəl/ ***
verdict *n* /ˈvɜːdɪkt/

Unit 3

advert *n* /ˈædvɜːt/ *
afford *v* /əˈfɔːd/ ***
architecture *n* /ˈɑːkɪˌtektʃə/ **
available *adj* /əˈveɪləbl/ ***
balcony *n* /ˈbælkəni/ *
bungalow *n* /ˈbʌŋgəˌləʊ/ *
ceiling *n* /ˈsiːlɪŋ/ **
convenient *adj* /kənˈviːniənt/ **
converted *adj* /kənˈvɜːtɪd/
cosy *adj* /ˈkəʊzi/ *
cottage *n* /ˈkɒtɪdʒ/ **
deck *n* /dek/ **
décor *n* /ˈdeɪkɔː/
enormous *adj* /ɪˈnɔːməs/ ***
estate agent *n* /ɪˈsteɪt ˈeɪdʒ(ə)nt/
flat *n* /flæt/ ***
flat hunting *phrase* /ˈflæt ˌhʌntɪŋ/
fully-equipped *adj* /ˌfʊlɪrˈkwɪpt/
furnished *adj* /ˈfɜːnɪʃt/
futuristic *adj* /ˌfjuːtʃəˈrɪstɪk/
huge *adj* /hjuːdʒ/ ***
immaculate *adj* /ɪˈmækjʊlət/
inclusive *adj* /ɪnˈkluːsɪv/
landlord / landlady *n* /ˈlændˌlɔːd/ /ˈlændˌleɪdi/ **
let *v* /let/ ***
location *n* /ləʊˈkeɪʃn/ ***
luxurious *adj* /lʌgˈzjʊəriəs/
maintenance costs *n* /ˈmeɪntənəns ˌkɒsts/
modify *v* /ˈmɒdɪˌfaɪ/ **
moor *v* /mɔː/
narrow boat *n* /ˈnærəʊ ˌbəʊt/
old-fashioned *adj* /ˌəʊldˈfæʃnd/ **
rent *v* / rent *n* /rent/ *
round *adj* /raʊnd/ ***
semi-detached house *n* /ˌsemidɪˈtætʃt/
separate *adj* /ˈsep(ə)rət/ ***
service *v* /ˈsɜːvɪs/ **
share *v* /ʃeə/ ***
spacious *adj* /ˈspeɪʃəs/
studio flat *n* /ˈstjuːdiəʊ ˌflæt/
suit *v* /suːt/ ***
tenant *n* /ˈtenənt/ **
terraced house *n* /ˈterəst ˌhaʊs/ **
typical *adj* /ˈtɪpɪkl/ ***
unusual *adj* /ʌnˈjuːʒʊəl/ ***
view *n* /vjuː/ ***
warehouse *n* /ˈweəˌhaʊs/ **
way of life *phrase* /ˌweɪ əv ˈlaɪf/
well-decorated *adj* /ˌwelˈdekəˌreɪtɪd/
windmill *n* /ˈwɪndˌmɪl/

Unit 4

accountant / accountancy *n* /əˈkaʊntənt/ /əˈkaʊntənsɪ/ **
achieve *v* /əˈtʃiːv/ ***
aim *v* /eɪm/ ***
ambition *n* /æmˈbɪʃn/ **
argue *v* /ˈɑːgjuː/ ***
celebrate *v* /ˈseləˌbreɪt/ ***
charity *n* /ˈtʃærəti/ ***
clear *adj* /klɪə/ ***
competitive *adj* /kəmˈpetətɪv/ **
concerned *adj* /kənˈsɜːnd/ ***
confident *adj* /ˈkɒnfɪd(ə)nt/ **
consider *v* /kənˈsɪdə/ ***
contacts *n* /ˈkɒntækts/ ***
contemporary *adj* /kənˈtemp(ə)rəri/ ***
control *v* /kənˈtrəʊl/ ***
disappointed *adj* /ˌdɪsəˈpɔɪntɪd/ *
dreadful *adj* /ˈdredfl/ **
due (to do something) *v* /djuː (tə duː sʌmθɪŋ)/ ***
emotional *adj* /ɪˈməʊʃn(ə)l/ ***
end up *v* /ˌend ˈʌp/ ***
entire *adj* /ɪnˈtaɪə/ ***
event *n* /ɪˈvent/ ***
expect *v* /ɪkˈspekt/ ***
fund-raising *n* /ˈfʌndˌreɪzɪŋ/
get into *v* /ˌget ˈɪntuː/
glamorous *adj* /ˈglæmərəs/
graduate *v* /ˈgrædʒuˌeɪt/ *
grow up *v* /ˌgrəʊ ˈʌp/
history / historian *n* /ˈhɪst(ə)rɪ/ /hɪsˈtɔːriən/ ***
hope *v* /həʊp/ ***
independent *adj* /ˌɪndɪˈpendənt/ ***
intend *v* /ɪnˈtend/ ***
law / lawyer *n* /lɔː/ /ˈlɔːjə/ ***
linguist / linguistics *n* /ˈlɪŋgwɪst/ /lɪŋˈgwɪstɪks/ *
look around *v* /ˌlʊk əˈraʊnd/
medicine *n* /ˈmedsn/ **
move on *v* /ˌmuːv ˈɒn/
odd *adj* /ɒd/ **
parental consent *n* /pəˌrentl kənˈsent/
personal trainer *n* /ˌpɜːsnəl ˈtreɪnə/
pharmacist / pharmacy *n* /ˈfɑːməˌsɪst/ /ˈfɑːməˌsi/
physicist / physics *n* /ˈfɪzɪˌsɪst/ /ˈfɪzɪks/
physiotherapist / physiotherapy *n* /ˌfɪziəʊˈθerəpɪst/ /ˌfɪziəʊˈθerəpi/
prison *n* /ˈprɪzn/ ***
profession *n* /prəˈfeʃn/ ***
psychologist / psychology *n* /saɪˈkɒlədʒɪst/ /saɪˈkɒlədʒi/ **
qualification *n* /kwɒlifɪˈkeɪʃn/ ***
set up *v* /ˌset ˈʌp/
solicitor *n* /səˈlɪsɪtə/ **
special occasion *n* /ˌspeʃl əˈkeɪʒn/
statistician / statistics *n* /ˌstætɪˈstɪʃn/ /stəˈtɪstɪks/
successful *adj* / succeed *v* /səkˈsesfl/ /səkˈsiːd/ ***
surprise *n* /səˈpraɪz/ ***
take off *v* /ˌteɪk ˈɒf/
volunteer *v* /ˌvɒlənˈtɪə/ *
vote *v* /vəʊt/ ***
well-known *adj* /ˌwelˈnəʊn/ **

Communication activities

Student A

Unit 3, Speaking Ex 1 page 13

1 Read the instructions carefully. Don't show your information to student B.

You are an estate agent in Edinburgh. You have the following accommodation to offer students. You are going to receive a phone call. Be ready to answer the phone.

Accommodation	Location	Furnished	Facilities	Condition	Rent
1 A large room in a shared non-smoking house	Close to the shops in the city centre. Quite noisy	Yes	Shared bathroom and kitchen, garden, off-road parking	Clean and well decorated. But walls have been painted black	£300 per month
2 A country cottage	A village in the country, 15 km from the city centre	No	3 bedrooms, sitting room, large modern kitchen, large bathroom, garden and garage	Good	£800 per month inclusive
3 A room with host family in semi-detached house for non-smoker	In a quiet road 4 km from the city centre	Yes	Beautifully furnished and spacious	Very good	£400 per month with breakfast and dinner
4 A 3rd floor flat in modern block	10 minute walk to city centre	Yes	Separate shower room and kitchen. Parking space	Needs decorating	£450 per month

Unit 5, Vocabulary Ex 1 page 19

Five minute challenge

HOW TO PLAY

1. Read the clues. You have to guess as many words as possible in five minutes.
2. After five minutes stop and check the answers with your partner. Add up your scores.
3. Find out who scored the most points in your class.
   Example:
   G: Accepted into a college or team = **g**et in

ANSWERS FOR STUDENT B

Nice and easy: relax, unusual, view, wonderful

Can you take it?: protect, routine, set up, volunteer

Top linguists: immaculate, linguist, unwind, warehouse

Nice and easy (1 point)

A: extremely bad
E: very large
H: something that you do often
M: extremely unhappy

Can you take it? (2 points)

B: a house that is on one level
E: an act of getting away
M: a game where players compete
O: someone who is competing against you

Top linguists (3 points)

C: someone who spends a lot of time watching TV
D: a pleasant but not too strong taste
D: the style of decoration in a house
I: including all costs

Listening scripts

Unit 1 My life

Listening script 01

Reading text from page 3

Listening script 02

(S = Sarah; J = Jenny)

S: Hello?

J: Hello, Sarah, is that you? It's me – Jenny.

S: Oh hi Jenny! Why are you whispering? Where are you?

J: I'm phoning from the health farm and I don't want anyone to overhear.

S: Oh dear – how are you getting on?

J: Well, I've been here for seven days and it feels like 17. At first I thought it was going to be great but in fact it's absolutely awful.

S: Oh no, why?

J: Well, you won't believe this but we're forced to get up at six o'clock in the morning and go for a run around the lake before breakfast.

S: Oh, poor you! That sounds awful.

J: And if that wasn't bad enough, all we get for breakfast is grapefruit and water.

S: You're joking! You can't survive on that.

J: I don't think I am surviving. And then we're expected to go to at least two exercise classes before a really miserable lunch.

S: Really? What do you have for lunch then?

J: A bowl of soup and a glass of carrot juice.

S: Any bread?

J: Not a chance.

S: Well, do you get a decent meal in the evening?

J: I suppose dinner's slightly better. We usually get a baked potato and a green salad.

S: Oh well, never mind. Not much longer to go.

J: Yes, I'm leaving in a couple of days. Can't wait.

S: Anyway, how are you feeling?

J: Oh absolutely wonderful. I've lost three kilos.

S: Oh, it's all been worthwhile then ...

Unit 2 Who needs fame?

Listening script 03

(I = Interviewer; S = Sue)

I: Sue, you've been writing articles about famous people for the last 20 years. What do you think the advantages of being famous are?

S: Well, I think the first is a sense of achievement, which is so important to them. They've done it. They've got to the **top of their tree** and so they feel good about themselves. Then, of course famous people usually, but not always, make a lot of money, so they have no financial worries, especially sports people, film stars, fashion designers, singers and others in the entertainment industry. Often famous people don't even have to spend money on clothes as fashion designers give their latest designs to them. When stars are seen wearing a designer's clothes, it's great free advertising. And of course you can always get a table at a restaurant or a ticket for a football match if you're famous.

I: Anything else?

S: The famous are always attracted to each other so I suppose you get to meet some interesting people.

I: What about the downsides?

S: I think there are several of these. Firstly, you have no privacy. Journalists and photographers follow you everywhere, taking pictures and writing stories about you. Then of course, there's the threat of being followed by crazy people or having your child kidnapped, so security is a big issue. John Lennon is perhaps the most famous example of a star whose security wasn't good enough. Then there's the constant pressure on you to **live up to the expectations of the public** – if you're a film star you're expected to appear glamorous and exciting all the time. Finally, they often find it hard to make friends and have a normal relationship with someone. Famous people seem to be getting together and **breaking up** all the time.

I: So, would you like to be famous yourself?

S: Oh, let me see ... erm ... I think just for a month to see what it feels like – I'd probably hate it after that!

I: Why do you think some people are so desperate to become famous?

S: That's a very interesting question. I often get this feeling that most of the people I've interviewed for magazines are really trying to compensate for some problems they think they have with their character. They **suffer from low self-esteem**; maybe they feel they weren't really loved by their parents, or they were **bullied at school**. So then there's this big desire to prove themselves and they have this **terrific drive to succeed**.

Listening script 04

advantage article exciting famous journalist magazine pressure privacy public terrific worry

Listening script 05

Reading text from page 7

Unit 3 A place to live

Listening script 06

Reading text from page 11

Listening script 07

(F = Fiona; M = Maria)

F: ... and I really don't mind if you want to stay a bit longer.

M: Well I've found some adverts on the Internet. Some of them look quite interesting.

F: Oh? Let's have a look.

M: I can't afford it if the rent's more than about £400 a month really.

F: £400 a month? Well, you should be able to find something for that. You might have to travel a bit.

M: Well that's the thing. I don't want to spend time travelling, waiting for buses in the cold. I want to be able to go into the university easily and be close to the centre.

F: Well yes, I can understand that. I mean Edinburgh's a great city and there's lots going on.

M: That's what I think. Anyway, have a look at these.

Listening script 08

(F = Fiona; M = Maria)

F: OK. How about this flat? Central location, one double bedroom, bathroom, hall, lounge, fully-equipped kitchen.

M: That sounds nice, Where is it?

F: It's in Old Town.

M: That's nice. And how much is it?

F: £500 per month I'm afraid.

M: Ooh. That's too much.

F: Yes, it sounds a bit expensive. How about this one in New Town? That's not as central as Old Town, but it's still a nice area, though. Listen. £400 per calendar month, a studio flat fully-furnished and equipped. Bright double-windowed room with sofa bed. Separate kitchen and shower room.

M: Hmm. So it has a sofa bed because there isn't a separate bedroom. Is that right?

F: Yes. What do you think?

M: I'd rather have a separate bedroom really.

F: Yes. OK. Let's have a look at this one. Room to let. Single fully-furnished bedroom to rent in spacious and immaculate city centre flat off Princes Street.

M: Does that mean it's to share?

F: Yeah. But it's in an excellent location. And listen to this: lounge, dining room, bathroom and kitchen. The building even has a swimming pool! Wow! And it's only £350 per month.

M: But, of course, it's sharing. It sounds nice and it's much cheaper than the others, but I really don't want to share.

F: Let's have another look. Leith Walk with stunning view. Bedroom, sitting room, oh but it says non-smoker. That's no good for you is it?

M: Unfortunately not.

F: Couldn't you give up?

M: No! I'm not going to give up smoking just to find a flat! ... Let's go back to that one to share with the swimming pool.

F: What was it? Ah yes! Single fully-furnished bedroom to rent in spacious flat ... off Princes Street ... Building has a swimming pool ...

M: Yes, that's the one.

F: Views of Edinburgh castle! Of course, it depends on who you're sharing with.

M: Absolutely.

F: But I think it's worth having a look at. It sounds fantastic. And it could be nice, having other people around. You don't have to be good friends with them.

M: That's true. It would be someone to talk to. OK I'll have a look!

F: Good idea. After all you like swimming don't you ... ?

Unit 4 Life changes

Listening script 09

Reading text from page 14

Listening script 10

(I = Interviewer, P = Peter, M = Maria, J = James, S = Sophie)

Peter

I: Well, Peter, does it feel strange to read about what you hoped for when you were 18 now that you're 28?

P: Yeah, I guess it does in a way. I'm not so confident about the future now as I was when I first started college.

I: Any particular reason?

P: When you're 18, you don't think anything is going to get in your way, but you learn there's a lot you can't control.

I: Such as?

P: Well, the way you work, for one thing. I work for a computer company and people are always telling me what to do. So I've decided I'm going to set up my own business. In the next five years I hope that I'll be rich and successful, but I know that's going to take a lot of hard work to achieve.

Maria

I: So Maria, you were worried about getting a good job and going to university. What's happened to you since then?

M: Yeah, it was difficult at first. Sure, I had to work hard to get to university, and then I began to work as a solicitor for a big company. Five years ago I got married, and now I've got two children. My husband and I are saving hard, and intend to send them both to college, to make things a bit easier for them.

I: And what do you do?

M: I still work as a solicitor. My husband is studying to be a lawyer, and so we're hoping to start our own company in the future.

I: Good luck to you both!

James

I: James, ten years ago you wanted to become a doctor …

J: Yeah, but unfortunately I didn't get the grades I needed.

I: So what did you do then?

J: Well, I was very disappointed, but I just had to move on and do something else with my life. So I took a year off and worked as a volunteer on an aid programme. That made me realise how important fundraising is for medical charities. So that's what I do.

I: Can you explain a bit more about what you actually do?

J: I contact likely donors, put forward our case and organise big fundraising events.

I: So have you achieved any of your ambitions?

J: Well, I always said I wanted to help other people, so I guess so.

I: And what about the future?

J: My fiancée and I intend to get married next year.

I: Congratulations!

Sophie

I: Are you still a dancer, Sophie?

S: Well, I soon realised that I would never make it to the top of my profession as a dancer, so I looked around for something else.

I: And?

S: And I found I could make a lot of money as a personal trainer.

I: What do you mean?

S: I mean someone who advises people on their physical fitness, and develops programmes for them to follow. Dance exercises are a great way to keep fit, you know. Next year I intend to produce my own DVD and book, and I hope it'll be successful.

I: And did you ever get to New York?

S: Only for a holiday!

Listening script 11

Doctor, medicine, accountant, accountancy, historian, history, linguist, linguistics, pharmacist, pharmacy, psychologist, psychology, physicist, physics, physiotherapist, physiotherapy, solicitor, law, statistician, statistics, teacher, teaching

Unit 5 Review

Listening script 12

(P = Paul Logan; M = Megan Robinson; J = Johnny Wade)

P: … So Johnny, where did you find the inspiration for your new TV series?

J: I create a lot of characters from conversations I overhear in pubs and bars and on the bus. I also love listening to people's conversations on mobile phones. After listening to them I always make a note of what they said.

P: Well, I guess we'll all have to be careful about what we say on the phone in case Johnny's around. The reviews say that your new series is by far the funniest new show this year, and we're all looking forward to seeing it. It's due to start next week. Ladies and gentlemen – Johnny Wade. Our next guest in the studio is Megan Robinson. For years we've gone without winning a major tennis title. Now we have someone who's tipped to win Wimbledon one day. She's just won her first singles tournament in Melbourne. It's the Maria Sharapova of British tennis, Megan Robinson. Is this the first time that you two have met?

M: Yes it is.

J: Yeah, but I watched your final in Melbourne on TV and thought you were fantastic. Your tennis was pretty good too.

M: Oh thanks Johnny.

P: Er, right Megan, many congratulations on your recent success. What was that like?

M: Well it was by far the biggest tournament I've ever been in. There are some strong players out there and there's always an element of luck, really, so on the day, in the final I was just a bit luckier than my opponent.

J: Not true, not true.

P: Yeah, well it's a fantastic achievement at the age of 18. Do you play Johnny?

J: Well, I've tried occasionally but I can't hit the ball. Maybe I'd better have some lessons. How about it Megan?

M: Mmm. Technique is the most important thing. I could give you a few tips if you like …

P: But you must have a tough training schedule which keeps you busy?

M: Yeah, I usually train for a couple of hours with my coach in the mornings before doing an hour in the gym to build up my strength. After that I try to have a light lunch and then have a bit of a knockabout with my doubles partner. Then finally I go for a jog for about 30 minutes. It's tough but I enjoy it.

J: Wow, what a woman!

P: What about your lifestyle though, that must have a downside?

M: I suppose the worst thing is what I can and can't eat. I really need to be a bit lighter than I am at the moment. It would make me faster on court.

J: But you're gorgeous as you are!

P: All right. So, what happens next for you?

M: I intend to have a short break, maybe a week or so and then I hope to get right back into training ready for the grass court season which is coming up.

J: Say Megan, I've got an idea for a series about tennis players. Maybe we could get together so you could fill me in on some background.

M: I'm sure I could. I've got some spare time at the moment …

P: Well tonight I've been talking to …

J: Hang on I've got a pen somewhere. Yeah, here it is. What's your phone number?

P: Megan Robinson

M: Its 0203 …

P: … and Johnny Wade

J: Do you like Italian food? There's this great little place I know near …

P: Time for another record I think. Here's the latest release from …

Listening script 13

Song from page 20

Communication activities

Student B

Unit 3, Speaking Ex 1 page 13

1 Read the instructions carefully. Don't show your information to student A.

You are the accommodation officer at the Castle School of English, Edinburgh. You have to find accommodation for these students. You are going to telephone an estate agent. When you and Student A are both ready to begin, you must start the telephone conversation.

Name and nationality	Age	Accompanied by:	Reason for coming to the Castle School	Other information
1 Kenji, from Osaka in Japan	24	His wife, Kumiko, and their new baby son	Is being paid by his company to attend a language course	Smokes. Doesn't want to be in the city centre. Would like a garden
2 Francesca, from Turin in Italy	18	Alone	Taking a year off before university to learn English	Wants to share. Wants to be in the city centre. Doesn't have much money
3 Wen Ling, from Shanghai, China	22	Alone	Wants to go to Edinburgh university but has to improve her English first	Wants to live in a quiet area. Doesn't have much money. Doesn't mind sharing
4 Ahmed, alone. from Cairo, Egypt	25	Alone	Wants to improve his English in order to get a better job	Smoker. Wants to live alone. Needs somewhere to park his car

Unit 4, Speaking Ex 2 page 17

Answers to questionnaire
Mostly As: You aren't independent at all. Try making decisions for yourself sometimes!
Mostly Bs: You are quite independent but you also like to take advice from others.
Mostly Cs: You are very independent, but maybe you should get advice from others sometimes, too.

Unit 5, Vocabulary Ex 1 page 19

Five minute challenge

HOW TO PLAY

1 Read the clues. You have to guess as many words as possible in five minutes.

2 After five minutes stop and check the answers with your partner. Add up your scores.

3 Find out who scored the most points in your class.

Example:
G: Accepted into a college or team = **g**et in

ANSWERS FOR STUDENT A

Nice and easy: awful, enormous, habit, miserable

Can you take it?: bungalow, escape, match, opponent

Top linguists: couch potato, delicate, décor, inclusive

Nice and easy (1 point)

R: rest and become calm
U: not normal, common or ordinary
V: things you can see from a place
W: extremely good

Can you take it? (2 points)

P: keep someone safe
R: your usual way of doing things
S: start something such as a business
V: someone who works without expecting to be paid

Top linguists (3 points)

I: completely clean and tidy
L: someone who studies languages
U: begin to relax
W: a big building where goods are stored

Module 2
Relationships

Unit	Topic	Language study	Vocabulary	Main skills
1 **Family ties** pages 34–37	• Can your birth order change your personality? • Networks (Family and friends)	• Talking about the past and present (past simple and present perfect)	• Describing character	• **Reading:** summarising key information • **Listening:** completing a network diagram • **Speaking:** describing family and friend networks
2 **Neighbours** pages 38–41	• Neighbours from hell • My housemates are slobs!	• Degrees of politeness and formality	• Describing antisocial behaviour	• **Listening:** checking predictions • **Reading:** listing particular information • **Pronunciation:** sentence stress • **Speaking:** resolving disputes • **Writing:** a note
3 **Partners** pages 42–45	• Is it worth it? (Relationship issues) • A radio programme (Phone-in)	• Giving advice (*should, might think about, If I were you*)	• Phrasal verbs: relationships	• **Reading:** identifying key information • **Listening:** identifying details of a problem • **Speaking:** discussing and agreeing advice • **Writing:** an advice email
4 **Troubles** pages 46–49	• The twelfth day of July (Conflict in Northern Ireland) • How do you deal with conflict?	• Verb + preposition	• Describing conflict • Ways of dealing with conflict	• **Reading:** understanding a timeline; identifying key information • **Speaking:** discussing the results of a questionnaire • **Listening:** completing lists

RELATIONSHIPS

1 Family ties

LEARNING AIMS

- Can talk about the past and present
- Can describe character
- Can describe relationships with family and friends

Lead-in

1 Work with a partner. Which of these statements do you agree with? Discuss your ideas.

- It's better to come from a big family. You can learn a lot from your brothers and sisters.
- Parents are always stricter with their oldest child.
- If you're an only child it's much harder to make friends later on in life.
- Middle children are always left out. It's better to be the oldest or youngest child.

2 What are the best and the worst things about having brothers and sisters? Is it better to be an only child?

Reading

1 **14** Read the text about birth order on page 35 and answer these questions.

1 What is birth order?
2 Why is birth order important?
3 Why do middle born children try to escape from the family?
4 Why do we choose friends that have the same birth order?
5 In what ways is it useful to know about birth order?

2 Match these headings to the paragraphs in the text.

a The effects of birth order on the characteristics of children ☐
b How birth order influences our choice of friends and who we marry ☐
c The advantages of knowing about birth order ☐
d What birth order is, and what psychologists claim about it ☐

3 Are these statements true or false according to the text? If they are false, explain why.

1 Your personality is decided by your birth order. ☐
2 Oldest children like breaking rules. ☐
3 Middle children may feel left out. ☐
4 Youngest children don't like being with other people. ☐
5 Only children may seem older than they are. ☐
6 Oldest children are likely to have other first borns as friends ☐
7 Birth order psychology can help in business. ☐

CAN YOUR BIRTH ORDER *change your personality?*

1 What makes you the kind of person that you are? Is it your personality, your background and experience, what star sign you are, or just luck? According to an astonishing new claim by some psychologists, your birth order – whether you're the oldest, middle, youngest, or an only child – also has a significant influence on your personality, and how you relate to your family.

2 What are the typical characteristics of children in different positions in the family? According to Dr Kevin Leman in *The New Birth Order Book*, if you're obedient, a high achiever, status conscious, and if you like to please your parents but don't like taking risks, you're probably a first born. You're also likely to be in a responsible job, possibly a teacher, a priest or even a politician. Middle children often feel the opposite of their older brothers and sisters – that they don't have a role in the family. They like taking risks and try to escape by making lots of friends. Being quite independent, they often get jobs far away from their families, sometimes in another country. They're usually very ambitious and successful. If you are the youngest, you're probably affectionate, unselfish, sociable, a rebel and you like to entertain people. Many famous comedians are last borns. If last borns end up in conventional jobs, for example as lawyers or scientists, they are likely to be radical or rebellious members of their professions. What about if you've behaved like an adult since you were very young, set yourself high standards; you're good at motivating yourself and feel more comfortable with people older or younger than yourself? Then you're probably an only child.

3 Interestingly, we often choose friends of the same birth order as ourselves, since they have the same desires, the same approach to life and often the same problems. However, while many people choose a partner of the same birth order, according to Dr Leman, the most successful marriages are those of birth order opposites. This is exactly what the old saying says: 'opposites attract'.

4 Knowing about birth order is not just interesting, it's also useful. Dr Leman believes that knowing why you behave in a certain way can help you to understand your relationships with your family and the people around you better. And it helps in business, too. For example, knowing your clients' birth orders can help you to negotiate with them more successfully. Does birth order affect our personality? According to Dr Leman, the answer is 'yes'.

4 Find words and phrases in the text which mean:

1. a statement that something is true (paragraph 1) ______________
2. concerned about your place in society (paragraph 2) ______________
3. someone who likes to break the rules (paragraph 2) ______________
4. the usual type, not new or different (paragraph 2) ______________
5. way of thinking about something (paragraph 3) ______________
6. try to reach an agreement through discussion (paragraph 4) ______________

5 Complete this summary of the birth order theory. Write *Oldest child*, *Middle child*, *Youngest child* and *Only child* in the correct boxes.

mature, self-motivated, ambitious, confident	obedient, responsible, cautious, hard-working	risk-taking, ambitious, independent, successful	affectionate, unselfish, sociable, rebellious
______________	______________	______________	______________

6 Work with a partner. Discuss whether you and your family conform to the birth order theory.

LANGUAGE STUDY

Talking about the past and present

Past simple and present perfect

1 Read these sentences and answer the questions.

a *I always* ***wanted*** *to please my parents when I was a child.*
b *My position in the family* ***has affected*** *me.*

Which sentence:

1 talks about the past, and the time up to now?
2 talks about a completed time in the past?
3 has a verb in the present perfect?
4 has a verb in the past simple?
5 has a time phrase which tells us about the time of an event?

2 Which of these time words and phrases go with the past simple, and which with the present perfect? Which can be used with both tenses?

always	ever	for (two days)	just	last year	never	since	two weeks ago	when I was a child

Grammar reference page 58

3 Complete these sentences with the past simple or present perfect form of the verbs.

1 When I was a child I (behave) _______________ very well on the whole. I always (do) _______________ what my parents (tell) _______________ me to do.
2 I don't get on well with my brother. When we were children we (not play) _______________ together. I (not see) _______________ him for a long time.
3 I (live) _______________ at home since I was a child. I can't imagine moving into a flat by myself.
4 I (just come back) _______________ from a trip to the USA with a friend. We (have) _______________ a great time.
5 I (never visit) _______________ my cousins because they live in a different country.

4 Work with a partner. Discuss which of the sentences in Ex 3 are true, untrue or partly true for you.

Describing character

Vocabulary

1 Match the words in the box to the definitions.

affectionate	arrogant	bad-tempered	generous	insensitive	narrow-minded
reliable	sociable				

Someone who:

1 you can trust to do what you ask or expect of them _______________
2 shows that they love or care about someone _______________
3 doesn't notice or care about other people's feelings _______________
4 thinks they are better or more important than other people _______________
5 is interested in meeting people or doing things with other people _______________
6 isn't interested in ideas that are different from their own _______________
7 is prepared to give more time or money to others than is expected _______________
8 easily becomes annoyed or angry _______________

2 Which adjectives in Ex 1 normally have positive meanings, and which normally have negative meanings? Do you know any more character adjectives?

3 The following gossip was heard in a newspaper office. What adjectives in Ex 1 would you use to describe the behaviour of the people being talked about?

1 He told other people about his intention to fire me before he had spoken to me. I was really upset about this. ______________
2 He got so angry with his secretary that he threw a book at her. She was only one minute late. ______________
3 As soon as he got promoted he went around telling everyone that he was obviously the only person for the job! ______________
4 He spent hours going through my proposal just to help me out. He even offered to help me plan the presentation. ______________
5 Sarah has never been ill. She always arrives on time and finishes all her work. How does she do it? ______________
6 Have you spoken to the new assistant manager? He really likes meeting and chatting with people. ______________

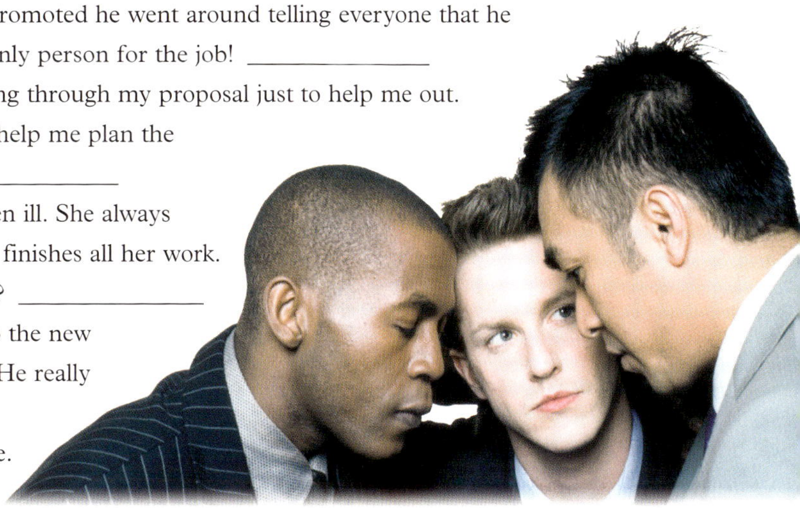

Listening and speaking

Networks

1 Look at Dave's network of family and friends. Who is his closest friend? Who doesn't he get on well with in his family?

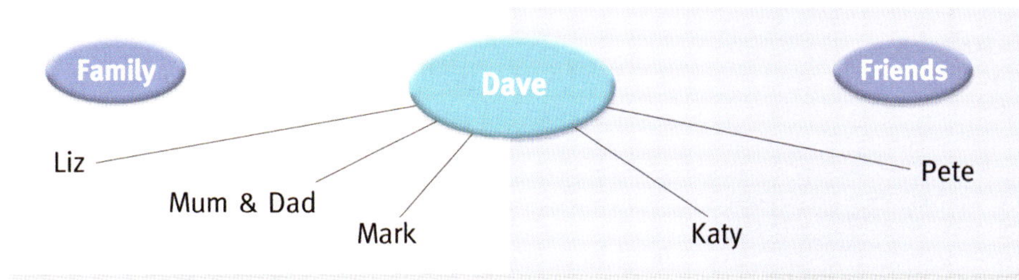

2 15 Listen and complete Amanda's network with the names in the box.

Adam	Helen	Kerri	Laura	Mum	Nick

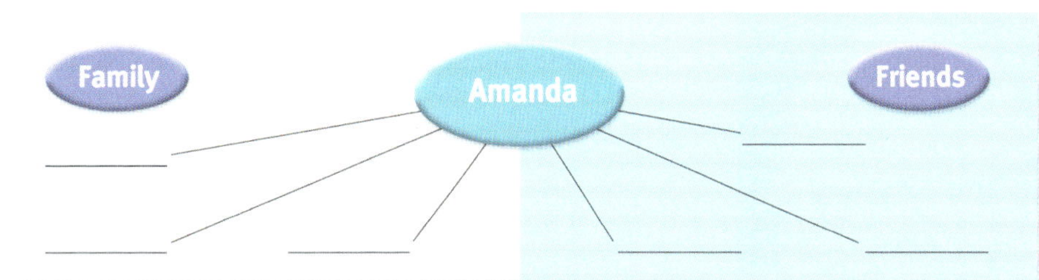

3 Draw your own friends and family network. Include at least six other people.

4 Work with a partner. Show each other your networks and talk about your relationship with the people. Include this information:

- How you met them
- How long you have known them
- How often you see them / speak to them
- How close they are to you
- Which of their qualities you like or dislike

CD-ROM For more activities go to **Relationships Unit 1**

2 Neighbours

LEARNING AIMS

- Can understand degrees of politeness and formality
- Can describe antisocial behaviour
- Can resolve disputes

Lead-in

1 Work with a partner and describe your neighbours. Include this information:

- Who they are
- What they do
- How you get on with them
- Whether you've ever had any problems with them

Neighbours from hell

Listening and vocabulary

1 You are going to listen to a news item from a local radio station in Brighton. Match these words from the news item to the definitions.

1	sue	a	period of time instead of prison when your behaviour is checked
2	obsessed	b	possible or likely
3	swear	c	annoying or unpleasant behaviour towards someone
4	conviction	d	use deliberately offensive or unpleasant language
5	harassment	e	make a legal claim against someone
6	potential	f	decision by a court that someone is guilty of a crime
7	probation	g	thinking about something all the time in a way that others consider extreme

2 Work with a partner. Look at the photo and the words in Ex 1. Predict what you think the news story will be about.

3 16 Listen to the story and check your predictions.

4 Listen again and tick what Mr Rogers did to the Thomases.

1 Swear at their guests ☐
2 Throw old furniture into their garden ☐
3 Break their bicycle ☐
4 Throw bits of wood at their windows ☐
5 Sing insulting songs ☐

5 Answer these questions.

1 Why did Mr Rogers start this 'campaign of hate'?
2 What happened in December?
3 What information do the Thomases have to give to potential buyers of their house?
4 What are the Thomases planning to do if they lose money on the sale of their house?

6 Work in a small group and discuss these questions.

1 The news item tells us the Thomases' version of events. What do you think Mr Rogers' side of the story is?
2 How do you think the Thomases could have avoided this problem?
3 How would you resolve this problem so that both sides are happy?

LANGUAGE STUDY

Degrees of politeness and formality

1 Look at these requests. Which one is the most polite and formal? Which one is the most informal?

Can you move your car? *Could you move your car?* *I was wondering if you could move your car.*

2 Look at the examples in Ex 1 again. When we want to be more polite or formal do we use present tense verb forms or past tense verb forms?

3 If we want to be particularly polite or formal we can use an introductory phrase, and sometimes this changes the word order of the rest of the sentence. What is the introductory phrase in the examples in Ex 1?

4 Compare these sentences. Which sentence is more sensitive?

I'm very sorry, but one of our guests parked in front of your house.
One of our guests parked in front of your house.

Grammar reference page 59

NOTE

It's important to be polite, but if you are too formal with friends, people may think you are being unfriendly or insincere.

5 Work with a partner. Look at these questions and statements. Which are the most and least polite / formal? Think about the use of past tense forms and introductory phrases. Discuss your ideas.

1 a I wondered if you would turn the music down.
  b Will you turn the music down?
  c Would you turn the music down?

2 a Can you explain why you are so angry?
  b Could you explain why you are so angry?
  c I was wondering if you could explain why you are so angry.

3 a I'd be very grateful if you'd stop shouting, please.
  b I'd like you to stop shouting, please.
  c Will you stop shouting, please?

4 a Would you mind if I organised a party?
  b Do you mind if I organise a party?
  c Can I organise a party?

5 a Is it alright if I invite some friends round?
  b I wonder if you would mind if I invited some friends round.
  c Would you mind if I invited some friends round?

6 What would you say in each situation? Discuss your ideas. If:

1 you felt hot in the classroom and the teacher was near the window
2 you saw a ten-year-old boy swearing at an old lady / man
3 you had a headache and your normally friendly neighbour was playing his electric guitar loudly
4 you were annoyed because a stranger wanted to tell you their life story on the bus

7 Complete these sentences with the phrases in the box. Sometimes there is more than one possible answer.

I apologise for (+-*ing*)	I'm afraid that	I'm sorry, but	Well, actually

1 ________________ I can't come this evening.
2 ________________ forgetting to ring you last night.
3 ________________ I haven't been able to finish tidying up.
4 ________________ not inviting you to my party.
5 ________________ I have an appointment with a lawyer this evening.
6 ________________ Mr Taylor isn't here at the moment.

We don't get on

Reading **1** 17 Read the magazine article and answer these questions.

1 Who does most of the housework?
2 What's a slob?
3 Who annoys Matt the most? Why?
4 Who's the most popular?
5 Who's going to stay in the house next year?

2 Make a list of the adjectives used to describe each person in the text.
Example: Carl: *untidy*

MY HOUSEMATES are slobs!

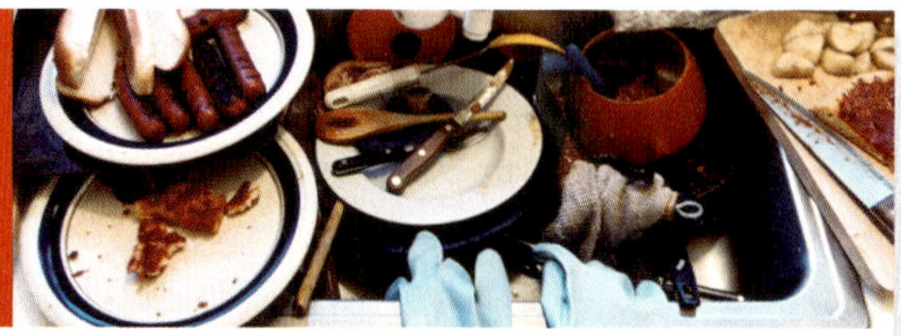

They met in their first year at university and decided to rent a house together to save money. Now, at the end of their second year, we asked students Matt, Jenny, and Carl to say what they thought of their housemates, and whether they'd stay in the same house for another year.

Last year we were all great friends, but it's amazing what you find out about each other when you live in the same house for a year! I mean for me, I always assumed that Carl and Jenny would clear up after themselves, and not leave the bathroom or kitchen in a mess – that sort of thing. I'm quite shocked at how untidy they are. I do most of the tidying up because they're complete slobs! I still like Carl. He's really generous, and he's got a great sense of humour. But he's impossible to live with. Jenny's OK, but she's a bit selfish. She does annoying things like invite her friends round late at night, and they make a lot of noise. She's the kind of person that never buys any bread, tea or coffee. When it runs out it's always me that has to do the shopping. I've decided to move out at the end of the year.

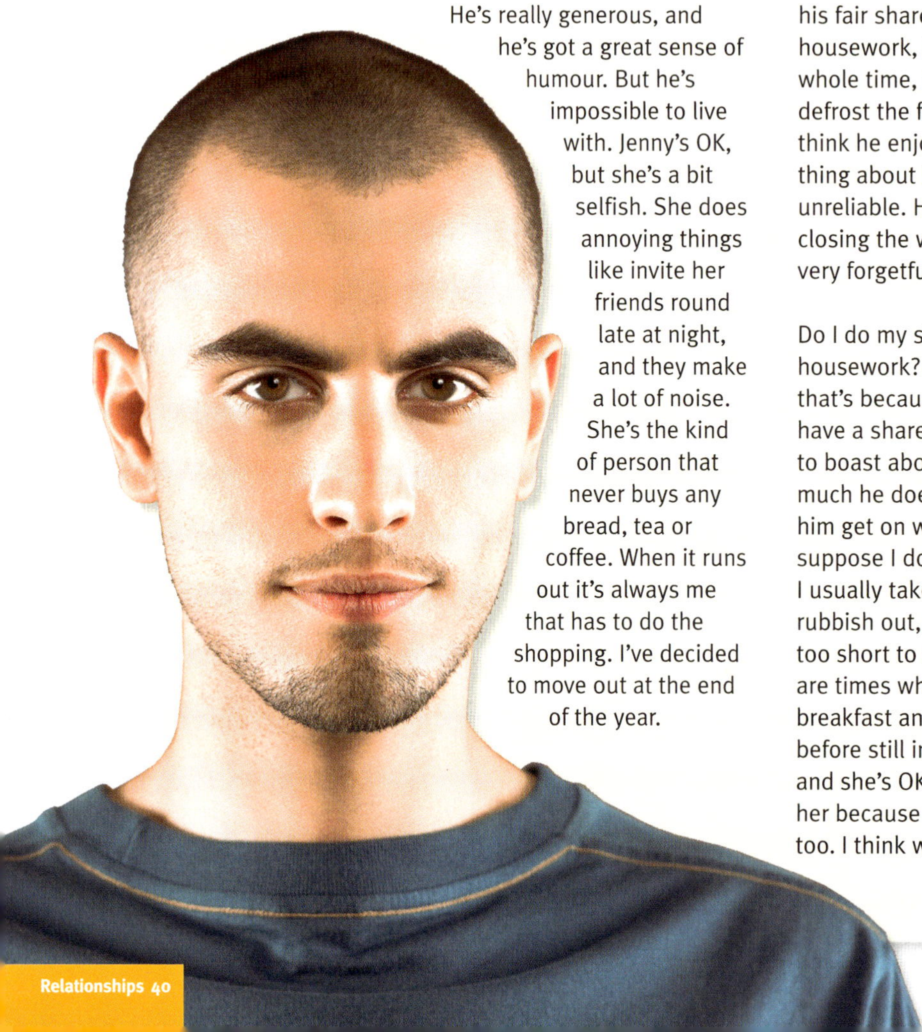

Since we moved in, Matt has become really bad-tempered and bossy. I think he likes to think that he's mature, but I think he takes life too seriously. It's true that he does more than his fair share of the housework, but he exaggerates and complains the whole time, too. He never notices when I do things like defrost the fridge or do the hoovering. Carl's great. I think he enjoys life and just gets on with it. The only thing about him that annoys me is that he's quite unreliable. He's always leaving the house without closing the windows or locking the door properly. He's very forgetful in that way.

Do I do my share of the housework? No, but that's because I don't have a share! Matt likes to boast about how much he does – so I let him get on with it. Well, I suppose I do a little bit. I usually take the rubbish out, but not until the bin is completely full! Life's too short to have arguments the whole time. Look, there are times when it depresses me to come down for breakfast and see Jenny's washing up from the night before still in the sink. But I just ask her to wash it up, and she's OK about it. Overall I get on really well with her because she's always cheerful, and I like her friends, too. I think we'll both stay here for another year.

3 Make a list of the jobs that each of the students does around the house.

4 Work with a partner and discuss these questions.

1 Would you share a house with any of these students? Why? / Why not?
2 What types of behaviour described in the article would annoy you?
3 What are the most important qualities of a housemate?

Pronunciation and speaking

1 **18** Listen and mark the stressed words. Which words are stressed and why?

Example: *Last night you left the bathroom in a mess.*

1 I always do your share of the housework.
2 Can you take the rubbish out tonight?

2 **19** Listen and repeat the sentences.

1 You never clear up after yourself.
2 You always leave your things lying around.
3 Please don't leave your dishes in the sink.
4 Could you remember to switch the lights off before you go out?
5 I wondered if you could defrost the fridge this week.

3 Work with a partner. You are going to discuss a complaint between two housemates who don't get on well. Use Ex 1 to help you choose a complaint. Plan your argument. Decide:

- What type of characters you are (bad-tempered, bossy, etc.)
- When the problem started and how long it's been going on
- Whether this is the first time you've discussed the problem
- Which of you will start the conversation and how the other will respond

4 Discuss your complaint.

5 Work with a partner. Two students have recently moved into a shared house together. Student A turn to page 61. Student B turn to page 64.

Writing

1 Write a note to a friend about the discussion you had in pronunciation and speaking Ex 4 from your point of view. Write about 150 words. Include this information:

- The background to the situation: what the problem was and who was involved
- What happened during the discussion
- How you feel about the result
- Your feelings about your housemate now

CD-ROM For more activities go to **Relationships Unit 2**

3 Partners

LEARNING AIMS

- Can give advice
- Can use phrasal verbs for relationships
- Can discuss relationship problems

Lead-in

1 Work in small groups. Which of these statements do you agree with? Discuss your ideas.

- You and your partner should both contribute equally to living expenses.
- Seeing your friends once a week is OK, but the rest of the time should be for your partner.
- It's very important to have similar hobbies or interests in a relationship.
- If you don't get on with your partner's family, the relationship will never work.

2 Discuss ways in which time, money and space can cause problems in a relationship.

Is it worth it?

Reading

1 **20** Read what Rob and Sara say about their relationship. In what ways do they get on well? What are their problems?

2 Work with a partner and discuss these questions.

1. Should Sara insist that Rob comes to her party?
2. If you were Rob, would you open a joint bank account with Sara?
3. What changes should they make to solve their problems?
4. Do you think Rob and Sara will stay together? Why? / Why not?

Sara When Rob and I met, we **hit it off** straight away. He makes me laugh, and we have a great time. When we first **got together**, I thought he was my ideal partner, but sometimes I wonder how serious he is about me. Last week I **fell out** with him about my birthday, which is in a few weeks. He knows I always have a big party. Of course I want him to be there, but he wants to go away with his friends that weekend, instead. He says they always go away together at that time. He wants us to go on holiday with them this year, too. When I told him it would be really romantic if it was just the two of us, he went very quiet. It's not that I don't like his friends. I do. We do lots of things together but I'd like to spend some time alone with him. I like staying at home, reading and listening to music. Rob likes those things too, but he also likes to go out more than me. Sometimes after our arguments I think about **breaking up** with him, but then he tells me something funny, and he feels like my perfect partner.

Rob I've been **going out** with Sara for nearly a year now. She's my first really serious girlfriend and most of the time we **get on** really well. She's pretty and she shares my sense of humour. We both like reading books and listening to music. But sometimes I feel like she wants to **take over** my whole life. She's annoyed with me about her birthday party. She wants me to be there, but I've known my friends since we were all little kids and we always go away together at this time of the year. I can't **let** them **down**, and she should understand that. Another thing is that when Sara invites her friends to our flat they take over the whole place. I mean it isn't very big and you can't **get away** from them. I'm afraid I don't like them very much. But that's not our main problem. We're supposed to be saving hard to buy a flat. I am but Sara's terrible with money. She wants us to have a joint bank account, but I'm worried that she'd spend it all. But I guess all couples have problems like this.

Phrasal verbs: relationships

Vocabulary

1 Match these phrasal verbs from the texts on page 42 to the definitions.

1	break up	a	escape from a person or place
2	fall out	b	like each other
3	get away	c	stop being friendly after an argument
4	get on	d	have a good relationship from the first meeting
5	get together	e	end a relationship
6	go out with	f	make someone disappointed
7	hit it off	g	take control of something
8	let down	h	have a romantic relationship
9	take over	i	to start a relationship

2 Put these statements about Helen and Jack's relationship in the correct order.

a A month later, they fell out after a big argument. All their friends were shocked. ☐

b They hit it off as soon as they met each other. 1

c They spent so much time together that Helen felt Jack was taking over her life. ☐

d They got on well and exchanged email addresses and phone numbers. ☐

e Helen told Jack that she needed time on her own to study for her exams. ☐

f They went out with each other for about six months. They went to weddings and parties together. They even went on holiday to Ibiza together. ☐

g Helen told Jack that she needed to get away from him, and they broke up. ☐

h Jack felt let down because he enjoyed spending time with her. ☐

i Jack tore up the photos he had of Helen, and got together with Liz. They had three children. Helen passed her exams, met a millionaire and moved to the USA. ☐

j They sent each other text and photo messages. Jack asked Helen out for a date. ☐

3 Work in pairs. You are going to invent relationship stories. Each of you must write down the following: the names of two famous people, a country, a building, a season, a piece of clothing, a job and a hobby. Use your partner's words to tell your story.

A radio programme

Listening

1 **21** Listen to Arabella Doyle's programme. Are these statements true or false?

1 This is a record request programme. ☐

2 Jane's problem is that her salary is much higher than her husband's. ☐

3 Jane has phoned Arabella to complain about her husband. ☐

4 In restaurants she gives her husband money under the table. ☐

5 They have a part-time nanny. ☐

6 Arabella thinks that Jane's husband doesn't want to be a house husband. ☐

7 Arabella advises Jane to ask her husband for money before they go out. ☐

8 Arabella advises Jane to open a joint bank account with her husband. ☐

2 Work with a partner and discuss these questions.

1 Do you agree or disagree with the advice Arabella gave Jane? Why?
2 What do you think Jane will do?
3 How would you feel if you were Jane's husband?

LANGUAGE STUDY

Giving advice

1 Compare these sentences. Which one is the advice Arabella gave Jane? Which word is used to give advice?

a *You could open a joint bank account.* b *Open a joint bank account.*

2 Look at the words and phrases used to give advice in these example sentences. Which advice phrase is followed by the *-ing* form? Which advice phrases are followed by the infinitive?

a ***You shouldn't*** *push him into being a house husband.*
b ***You might think about*** *giving him the money at home.*
c ***If I were you, I'd*** *do what you are doing.*

Grammar reference page 59

NOTE

Could, might think about and *if I were you, I'd* are all quite polite. You can use *should(n't)* when you want to be more direct or to give stronger advice.

3 Work with a partner. Imagine that you have three friends. One needs to lose weight, another needs to give up smoking, and the third needs to save money. Use the words and phrases in Ex 2 and think of advice that you could give them.

Speaking

1 Work in groups. Discuss the advice you would give to each of these people.

1 I've been offered the chance to set up a business as a DJ, but my parents refuse to help me buy the equipment. They want me to study law at university instead.

2 I broke up with my boyfriend six months ago. Now I want to meet someone new, but I don't know how.

3 My parents don't approve of my partner and won't invite us to their home.

4 My best friend is taking drugs and stealing things. What's the best thing to do?

5 I got a credit card last year and I used it to buy clothes, music, and presents for my wife and friends. I've now got a huge debt which I can't afford to pay off. I'm too scared to tell my wife.

6 I have just moved to a new country and I am finding it hard to meet people.

2 What do other groups think? Share your ideas with the rest of the class. Vote for the best piece of advice to each problem.

Writing

1 Read the email and answer these questions.

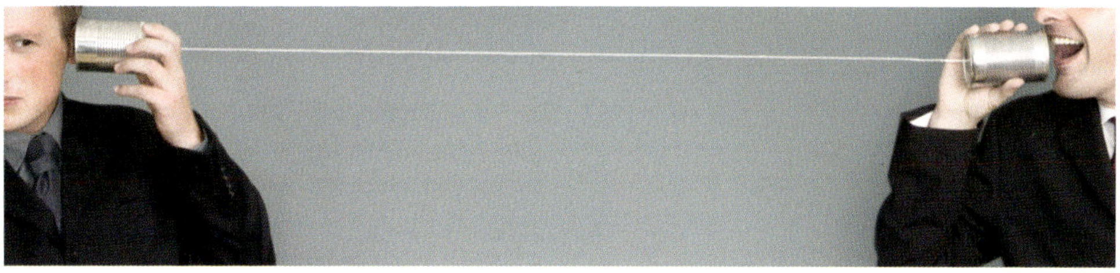

1 What's the relationship between Simon and Dave?
2 What does Simon do?
3 What is Dave's problem?
4 How old is Helen going to be next month?

Re:What shall I do?

To: dave.blackwell@tft.com
Cc:
Bcc:
Subject: Re: What shall I do?

Hi Dave,

I just got your email. It was great to meet up last month. Did we really drink that much? My journey back was fine, but I was a bit tired in my classes the next day. My lessons this term have been hard, but I'm still enjoying them. I told you about Nadia, didn't I? Well, I'm still going out with her - almost six months now and we're getting on really well. I'd love to introduce her to you. I'm sure you'd hit it off straight away.

I've been thinking about your dilemma. To be honest, I think you should just go to Sweden - you haven't seen your parents for ages! If your relationship can't last a 10 week break, it will never last. You can always call each other and email every day, and I know you don't really believe that she will run off with anyone else. If I were you, I'd plan a long trip together after you finish university. Plus Dave, if you don't go to Tom's summer party, he'll never forgive you!

By the way, are you going to Helen's birthday dinner next month? She's finally made it to her twenties. It would be great to see you there. Hopefully you will have made 'the right' decision by then!

Take care and see you soon.

All the best,
Simon

2 Which paragraph in the email:

a gives advice?
b greets Dave and catches up with news?
c asks about future plans?

3 Imagine your friend has a problem with a relationship (for example, about space, money or time). Write an email giving him / her advice. Remember to complete the address, subject and date details. Organise your message so that you:

- Greet your friend
- Give your friend some advice about the problem
- Ask about future plans

4 Work with a partner. Show him / her your email and ask them to guess what the problem is.

CD-ROM For more activities go to **Relationships Unit 3**

4 Troubles

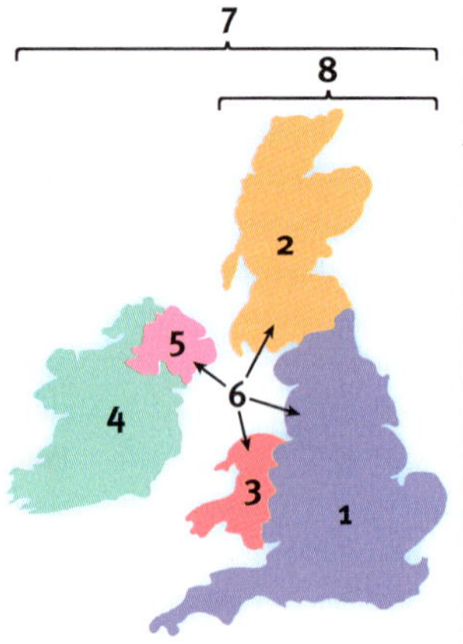

LEARNING AIMS

- Can recognise verb + preposition patterns
- Can discuss ways of dealing with conflict
- Can understand vocabulary to describe conflict

Lead-in

1 Look at the map and write the correct number next to the places in the box.

British Isles ____	England ____	Great Britain ____	Northern Ireland ____
Republic of Ireland ____	Scotland ____	Wales ____	United Kingdom ____

2 Look at the timeline. There are two cultural / political communities in Northern Ireland. What are they? Why have there been political differences and violence between them?

1603–1689

Elizabeth I, an English protestant queen, defeated Irish chiefs. Protestants were given land, especially in the north of Ireland.

1690–1915

On 12th July 1690 King William of England defeated an Irish / French Catholic army in Ireland.
18th–19th centuries: increasing control of Ireland by Britain. Poverty forced many Irish people to emigrate, especially during the famine of the 1840's. There were calls for 'home rule'.

1916–1969

The south of Ireland rebelled against Britain, and in 1921 a controversial agreement separated the mainly Catholic south from the mainly Protestant north of Ireland, which stayed a part of the United Kingdom. There was a civil war about the agreement. Economic growth was slow in the Republic of Ireland.

1969–1994

In Northern Ireland the conflict between Catholics and Protestants about political rights and jobs became violent. Many people were killed.

1994–now

New agreements have been made between the mainly Catholic (nationalist) and mainly Protestant (unionist) parties to share power in Northern Ireland.

This is a simplified timeline which only shows the main historical events

Reading and vocabulary

1 22 Read the extract from *The twelfth day of July* on page 47 and answer these questions.

1. What did Kevin and his friend do?
2. Which community do the McCoys belong to: Protestant (unionist) or Catholic (nationalist)?

2 Read the text again. Are these statements true or false?

1. Kevin's father is angry with his son for doing something so dangerous. ☐
2. Mrs McCoy believes that Kevin shouldn't start fights with the other community. ☐
3. Mrs McCoy believes Kevin's action will influence his brothers and sisters. ☐
4. Mrs McCoy advises Kevin to meet more protestants. ☐
5. Brede thinks that protestants can be good people. ☐
6. Mrs McCoy thinks that her sister is stupid. ☐

3 Work with a partner and discuss these questions.

1. What are Kevin's mother's and father's opinions about the violence that young people commit against the other community? Do they agree with each other?
2. Which of his parents has more influence on Kevin?
3. Do you think the McCoy's are a happy family? Why? / Why not?

4 Find words and phrases in the text which mean:

1. done in an unwilling way (line 05) ___________
2. stupid (line 09) ___________
3. hurt, or damaged (line 27) ___________
4. put something on a surface quickly and without care (line 30) ___________
5. surprised (line 32) ___________
6. stay with your own people (line 33) ___________

5 Complete these sentences so that they are true for you.

1. The last time I did something daft was when ___________________.
2. When ___________________, I was quite startled.
3. I would only attack someone if ___________________
4. I don't like ___________________ but I have a grudging respect for them.

The twelfth day of July by Joan Lingard is set in Belfast, Northern Ireland during 'the Troubles', a period of about 30 years that started in the late 1960s. This was a time of tension, hostility and violence between two communities, the mainly Protestant unionists (who want to stay in the United Kingdom) and the mainly Catholic nationalists (who want to leave the United Kingdom and unite with the Republic of Ireland).

The twelfth day of July

Kevin McCoy, a 14-year-old boy, and his friend have just got back home from a dangerous mission.

'I hear you were up to something last night after all, Kevin,' said Mr McCoy as he sat down to take his soup. But there was a grudging admiration in his voice and he said no more about it. He folded the newspaper so that he could read the greyhound* racing results.

'Daft idiots,' said Mrs McCoy as she ladled out the rest of the soup. 'Painting walls! Isn't that a carry-on for childer*? You and Brian are fourteen now, getting ready to be men.'

'But, Ma, we weren't painting an ordinary wall. We were protesting about what was on it.'

'Ould William*! He's not worth wasting paint on. If they want him on their walls let them have him. They're welcome.' She passed the steaming bowls of broth* to Brede who passed them round the table. 'As long as they don't come round painting his picture on my wall.'

'Women!' growled Kevin. 'They don't realise a man's got to fight for what he believes in.'

'Oh, we see that all right.' Mrs McCoy put the empty pot into the sink and ran water into it. 'But there's only a need to fight when you're being attacked. We've had enough fighting in this country to last us till the next century. So get on with your soup and don't think that you're smart just because you can slap paint on a wall. And it's not a suitable example to be setting for the wee* ones. Is that not right, Pete?'

Mr McCoy looked up, startled. 'Aye*, that's right.'

'You stick with your own, Kevin,' said his mother, 'and you'll come to less harm.'

'I'm sure some of the protestants must be quite nice,' ventured Brede. 'I read books about them and they don't sound all that bad.'

'Books!' said her mother. 'They don't tell the truth.'

'But didn't your sister Rose marry a protestant?'

'She did, but then she's soft in the head.'

'I've always liked her.'

'Maybe you're soft too,' said Kevin.

Brede turned and stuck out her tongue at him. They did not speak to one another for the rest of the afternoon.

The twelfth day of July by Joan Lingard, published by Penguin Books in association with Hamish Hamilton

Glossary

- * greyhound = a type of dog
- * Ould William = Old King William
- * broth = soup
- * These are dialect words used in Northern Ireland:
  aye = yes, childer = children,
  Ma = mother, wee = small

LANGUAGE STUDY

Verb + preposition

1 Many verbs are followed by prepositions. These verbs usually have more than one possible preposition.

*He **talked to** his son.*
*He **talked about** his son.*

After a verb:

a using a different preposition usually changes the meaning.
b two different prepositions can sometimes have the same meaning.
c the same preposition can sometimes have more than one meaning.

Match the verb + preposition combinations in these sentences to group 'a', 'b', or 'c'.

1 *I'm **thinking of** going to Paris for the weekend.*
*I'm **thinking about** going to Paris for the weekend.*

2 *I've always **dreamt of** having a sports car.*
*I would never **dream of** calling my boss by his first name.*

3 *I **heard about** the accident on the news last night.*
*I haven't **heard from** John for a while.*
*Have you **heard of** a film called 'Metropolis'?*

Grammar reference page 59

2 Find prepositions in the text on page 47 that follow these verbs.

Example: pass (something) *to*

1 protest _____
2 waste (something) _____
3 fight _____
4 read _____
5 speak _____

3 Work with a partner. Make correct sentences from this table.

I think everyone should read	to	things they think are wrong.
I would fight	about	clothes that I don't need.
I never pass my homework answers	about	the political history of their country.
I never speak	for	my classmates.
I sometimes waste money	to	my country if necessary.
I believe people should protest	on	strangers.

4 Work with a partner. Which of the statements in Ex 3 are true for you?

5 Complete these sentences with the correct prepositions. Sometimes there is more than one possible answer.

1 You can read a story __________ someone who is listening to you.
2 You can fight __________ someone __________ something you both want.
3 You can speak __________ a topic you are interested in.
4 You can protest __________ something you don't like.
5 You can pass the book __________ your partner.
6 You can waste time __________ something which is not important.

Speaking and listening

1 What happens when you disagree with someone? Find out what your reactions say about you by completing the questionnaire.

HOW DO YOU DEAL WITH conflict?

1 Someone expresses a different opinion from yours. How do you react?
- **a** have an argument with them
- **b** agree with them just to keep the peace
- **c** think carefully about your own views and perhaps change them

2 When discussing something with another person, it's clear that you can't agree. How do you feel?
- **a** superior because your views are obviously the most sensible
- **b** upset because you don't like arguments
- **c** quite calm. You are happy to agree to disagree

3 You've done something which has clearly annoyed someone else. What do you do?
- **a** the same thing again if you want to or need to
- **b** apologise because you don't like annoying people
- **c** discuss their feelings with them

4 Someone's done something which really annoys you. What do you do?
- **a** shout at them and tell them you'll never feel the same about them
- **b** nothing. It doesn't really matter
- **c** tell them about it

5 Two members of your family have had a big argument and are not speaking to each other. What do you do?
- **a** take sides with one of them and not speak to the other
- **b** stay on good terms with each of them by agreeing with what each one says about the other
- **c** talk to each of them and try to persuade them to make it up

2 Look at your answers. Are they mainly 'a', 'b' or 'c'?

3 Work with a partner. Discuss what you think your answers say about you.

4 **23** Listen to a specialist talking about conflict. What are the names of the three responses to conflict that she mentions?

1 ______________ 2 ______________ 3 ______________

5 Listen again. List the advantages and disadvantages for each way of responding.

Response	Advantages	Disadvantages
1		
2		
3		

6 Match responses 1, 2, and 3 to the 'a', 'b' and 'c' type answers in the questionnaire.

7 Do you agree with the specialist's views? Are there any other advantages and disadvantages for each response?

CD-ROM For more activities go to **Relationships Unit 4**

5 Review

Lead-in **1** Discuss these questions.

1 Do you think your first impressions of another person are important? Do you usually change your mind later?

2 Think about the first time you met a boyfriend, girlfriend or your best friend. What can you remember about your first meeting?

Vocabulary

1 **24** Listen to husband and wife Tony and Jacquie talking about when they first met. Make notes on their answers to these questions.

		Tony	Jacquie
1	When did they meet?		
2	At what event did they meet?		
3	What happened when they met?		
4	What was the other person wearing?		
5	What were their first impressions of the other person?		
6	What happened next?		
7	Where did they go for their first date?		

2 What are the differences between what Tony remembers and what Jacquie remembers?

3 Work in a small group. Discuss which three characteristics in the box you'd most like and three you'd most dislike for your partner.

> affectionate ambitious arrogant bad-tempered bossy cautious dishonest forgetful hard-working mature narrow-minded reliable responsible risk-taking self-motivated sensible sensitive sociable unselfish untidy

4 Complete the phrasal verbs with the correct form of the verbs in the box. You need to use some of the verbs twice.

> break fall get go hit let make

I first met my friend Ben when we started at secondary school. We (1) ________ it off immediately and we were always together. That was a long time ago. We're both married now. Over the years we've stayed friends. We (2) ________ out for a drink every now and then, and our families (3) ________ together occasionally for a day at the beach or something. Of course it's not like it was when we were kids, but we still (4) ________ on well. Once, though, we (5) ________ out over a girl. I (6) ________ up with her and a few days later Ben (7) ________ out with her! I thought that was really insensitive. Later, he apologised and we (8) ________ up. He's a good person. He's unselfish, he's got a great sense of humour, and he never (9) ________ you down. I like him a lot and I hope we'll always keep in touch.

Language study

1 Work in small groups. Read how to play 'On the right track' and play the game.

ON THE RIGHT TRACK

HOW TO PLAY

- Each person is a 'train', represented by a counter. The first player throws the dice and moves their counter (or 'train') along the track.
- Players then throw in turns. If a player lands on a square with a question (a 'station') they must use the words on it to make a sentence. The other players must decide if the sentence is correct. If it is, the player can pick up a point (a 'passenger'); if not, they don't get a point.
- When everyone has reached the finish (the 'terminus'), the player with the most 'passengers' is the winner.

3 I don't speak to …
6 Do you mind if I …
9 Have you ever …?
12 If I were you I'd …
16 For the last three years I …
18 Two weeks ago I …
22 I must apologise for …
25 Sometimes I waste money on …
29 I was wondering if you …
33 If I were you I wouldn't …
37 Is it alright if I …?
40 Recently I read something about …
44 You might think about …
48 Since I've been in this class I …
51 Have you heard of ….?
55 Would you mind ….?
58 When I was a child I …

Song

1 Work with a partner and discuss these questions.

1 How do people behave when they are in love?
2 How do they feel?
3 In what ways are they different from normal?

2 Find lines in the song which mean the same as these statements, and write the line numbers.

Example:
If his friends say bad things about his woman, a man in love will give them up. = *line 6*

1 He will give up his house and live outside, if his woman wants him to. ______
2 He will spend all his money on his woman, if necessary. ______
3 He won't be able to think about other things. ______
4 He will only see his woman's good points. ______
5 He won't realise if she's tricking him. ______
6 He won't look for another woman. ______
7 He will give up everything else for his woman. ______
8 He won't treat her badly. ______

3 Read the words of the song again. Find:

1 four words containing missing letters. What are the letters?
2 missing words at the start of three sentences. What are they?

When a man loves a woman

When a man loves a woman
Can't keep his mind on nothin' else
He'll trade the world for the good thing he's found
If she's bad, he can't see it
She can do no wrong
Turn his back on his best friend, if he puts her down

When a man loves a woman
Spend his very last dime*
Tryin' to hold on to what he needs
He'd give up all of his comforts
And sleep out in the rain
If she said that's the way it ought to be

Well this man loves a woman
I gave you everything I had
Tryin' to hold on to your high class love
Baby, please don't treat me bad

When a man loves a woman
Deep down in his soul
She can bring him such misery
If she plays him for a fool
He's the last one to know
Lovin' eyes can never see

When a man loves a woman
He can never do her wrong
He'd never want some other girl
Yes when a man loves a woman
I know how he feels
'Cause baby, baby, baby, you're my world

When a man loves a woman …

*dime = a small American coin

4 25 Listen to the song and discuss these questions.

1. Do you agree with the ideas in the song, or do you think they're exaggerated?
2. Do men and women behave in the same way when they're in love?
3. Would you behave like the person in the song? Why? / Why not?

5 Read the factfile and answer these questions.

1. What was Sledge's job before he became a professional singer?
2. What do some people call him?
3. What happened to him after his string of hits?
4. Does the factfile author think he was a 'one hit wonder'?

factfile

Percy Sledge was born in Alabama, in the south of the USA. He started singing as a teenager in church but he was soon singing in clubs. After graduating from high school he worked as a nurse, but continued singing in his free time. He signed up with Atlantic Records and in 1966 he released his biggest hit *When a man loves a woman* (written by Calvin Lewis and Andrew Wright) which topped the US charts. It's been popular ever since. It was, for example, used in the 1994 film *When a man loves a woman* starring Meg Ryan and Andy Garcia, and in a successful TV advertisement for jeans. Sledge had a string of rhythm and blues hits throughout the later 60s and he was nicknamed 'The golden voice of soul'. During the 1970s, however, his popularity decreased. Despite this, he's continued to tour the world and make records ever since then. Some people say he was a 'one hit wonder'. That's not really fair, but he will always best be remembered for his most famous song.

6 Work with a partner. Name pop stars who have produced a string of hits recently, and pop stars who've become 'one hit wonders'.

Speaking: preparing a dialogue

1 Work in groups of four or five. You are going to prepare a dialogue. Follow the instructions.

Step 1: Read about the characters

There are three people having an argument:

- Mrs Buxton (the mother): strict, a bit narrow-minded, very assertive and sometimes a bit bossy.
- Mr Buxton (the father): wants to keep the peace. He's very fond of his daughter and not quite as strict.
- Paula (their daughter): 15 years old and a bit rebellious and disobedient. She feels her parents are too strict and that she can look after herself.

Step 2: Read about the situation

It's midnight and Paula has just come home from a party at the other end of town. Her parents had told her to be back by 10.30 pm and they've been very worried about her.

Step 3: Write your dialogues

- At the top of a sheet of paper each person in your group writes the name of one of the characters and what this person says.
  Example: *Mrs Buxton: Where have you been?*
- Give your sheet of paper to the person sitting on your left.
- Read what the previous person wrote and then write the name of the next person to speak, and the next part of the argument. Pass your sheet to the person on your left.
- Continue writing the argument in this way until your teacher tells you to stop.

Step 4: Act out one of your dialogues

- In your group read all the arguments you have written and choose the best one.
- Check that you can understand everything, the grammar is correct, and that you have used the best words.
- Practise and then act out your dialogue to the rest of the class.

Extra practice

Unit 1

1 Complete the sentences with the words in the box.

affectionate arrogant bad-tempered cautious generous insensitive narrow-minded reliable selfish sociable

1 My aunt was never very ______________ towards her children. She didn't kiss or hug them much.
2 I think that only children are more likely to be ______________ because they don't have to share their toys with brothers and sisters.
3 Why was Ruth so ______________ yesterday? She shouted at everyone who spoke to her.
4 Katie is very ______________. She hates taking risks.
5 My grandfather could never see the other person's point of view, so I guess you'd say he was ______________.
6 That man is no better than anyone else so I don't know why he's so ______________.
7 Not many tutors are as ______________ with their time as Ken is.
8 Maureen and Brian have a party every month because they like being ______________.
9 It was ______________ of Susan to talk about her wedding plans in front of Becky when her marriage has just broken up.
10 Is John ______________ enough to do the job? I need someone who'll finish it on time.

2 Write three or four sentences to describe yourself and what your family think about you.

Example:
I think I'm affectionate and reliable. My family agree, but they also think that I'm sometimes a bit too independent, which is the reason I occasionally get into trouble. They may be right, but I'm ambitious and I want to succeed, so sometimes it's necessary to take a few risks.

____
____
____
____
____

3 Complete the table.

Verb	Past simple	Present perfect
affect	affected	
arrive		
behave		
go		
hear		have / has heard
know		
live		
make		
play		
see		
tell		
visit		

4 Complete the text with the past simple or present perfect form of the verbs.

Marcella's sister Bella (1 meet) ______________ her husband three years ago in Corfu and they (2 be) ______________ married for eighteen months. Marcella (3 be) ______________ a bridesmaid at their wedding but for months before it she (4 complain) ______________ because she (5 hate) ______________ the colour of her dress. She (6 never like) ______________ pink since her younger brother (7 tell) ______________ her that it made her look fat. Anyway, the wedding (8 be) ______________ wonderful. Bella (9 never think) ______________ she would get married so young. She's only twenty-three and now I (10 just hear) ______________ that she's going to have a baby next spring. The great thing is that she's really happy about it because she (11 always want) ______________ to have children.

Unit 2

1 Complete these sentences.

1 Eventually, Julie decided to *s*________ her boss for *h*________ because he kept shouting at her and bullying her in front of the customers.

2 Errol spends his whole time thinking about motorbikes. He rides them, he reads about them, and they're the only thing he talks about. I think he's *o*________.

3 Chris was so angry with Helen when she broke his CD player that he began to shout and *s*________ at her.

4 After the shop owner caught Sally taking the money, he took her to court and she was given a *c*________. She had to pay back £500 and she was put on *p*________ for a year.

2 Write character adjectives to describe these people.

1 Phil never puts his things away. He always leaves the house in a mess. ________

2 Fiona always behaves in a way that makes other people feel angry. ________

3 Lindsay always remembers to say 'please' and 'thank you'. ________

4 Neil's always giving orders and telling other people what to do. ________

5 Andy never remembers to do things. ________

6 Suzy is quite young, but she behaves in an adult way. ________

3 Rewrite these informal sentences so that they are more polite and formal. Use the words in brackets.

1 Turn off that radio, please. (I was wondering)

____

2 You can't park your car here. (I'm afraid that)

____

3 I need your telephone number. (I'd be very grateful)

____

4 Can you lend me a pen? (Would you mind)

____

5 You're too late for the film. (I'm sorry, but)

____

6 I forgot to post your letter. (I apologise for)

____

7 Why are you so bad-tempered today? (Could you explain)

____

8 I'd like to leave early today. (Is it alright)

____

4 Complete the text with the prepositions in the box.

on	out	round	up	with

Last weekend I invited a couple (1) ________ for an evening meal. They were people that I really get on well (2) ________. I spent ages tidying (3) ________ the house, making the beds, taking the rubbish (4) ________, hoovering the floor and clearing (5) ________ the mess in my room. I even went to the shops when I discovered I had run (6) ________ of coffee. When I had finished I finally sat down, turned (7) ________ the television and waited for them to arrive. After three quarters of an hour nobody had turned up, so I rang one of my friends. Apparently Jim was very depressed because he'd broken up with his girlfriend Sally, and she'd just moved (8) ________ after living with him for two years. He couldn't face coming (9) ________ for a meal. I was about to throw all the food away when Sally turned up!

Unit 3

1 Choose the correct alternative.

1 Paula and Greg *hit it off* / *got away* from the start because they both liked running.

2 Suzie and Colin *took over* / *got together* when they were in New York.

3 Jackie and Richard decided to *fall out* / *break up* and go their separate ways.

4 I haven't seen much of Jim since he started *going out* / *getting on* with Anna.

5 Linda *fell out with* / *let down* Pete really badly. He'd already bought their plane tickets when she decided to go on holiday with Martin instead.

6 Nicola and Andy *get on* / *get together* well. I've never seen them have an argument.

2 Complete these sentences with the correct form of the phrasal verbs in the box.

break up with	fall out	get on with
get together	go out with	hit it off
let down	take over	

1 Mike is very upset because he ______________ Ayesha last week.

2 I don't how Alison and Tim ever ______________. They don't share any of the same interests.

3 Janet and Jack ______________ from the moment they met and they've been together ever since.

4 Ann and her best friend ______________ because they both liked the same boy.

5 Joe felt ______________ by Karen because she only turned up twenty minutes after the film had started.

6 John ______________ his boss, although no one else in the office likes her.

7 It's obvious that Rachel ______________ Ian's life. He never does anything without asking her first!

8 Why won't Darina ______________ Don? It's obvious that she really likes him and he's asked her several times.

3 Respond to each of the problems. Use *should(n't), could, might think about,* or *If I were you.*

Example:
A: My head's aching.
B: *You should lie down for a while.*

1 A: It's my mother's birthday and I've no money to buy her a present.
B: ______________________________

2 A: My exam's next week and I haven't done any work for it.
B: ______________________________

3 A: My two best friends have quarrelled and aren't speaking to each other. How can I help?
B: ______________________________

4 A: I can't decide whether I should leave school and get a job or go to university.
B: ______________________________

5 A: My neighbour keeps on having really loud parties, and I can't sleep.
B: ______________________________

6 A: I'm really attracted to my best friend's boyfriend.
B: ______________________________

Unit 4

1 Complete these sentences with a preposition from the box. Sometimes there is more than one possible answer.

about at for of on to with

1 a I want to speak ___________ the conflict in Northern Ireland.
  b Yesterday I spoke ___________ my teacher about my progress.
2 a I heard ___________ your accident. I'm really sorry.
  b Yes, of course I've heard ___________ David Beckham!
3 a You must apologise ___________ Ken. He's very angry.
  b It's important to apologise ___________ your mistakes.
4 a I wasted my money ___________ a new laptop computer. It doesn't work!
  b I wasted my time ___________ the consulate. They didn't give me a visa.
5 a I don't agree ___________ you. You're wrong!
  b They agreed ___________ make an effort to get on with each other.
6 a I'm thinking ___________ buying some new boots.
  b Betty is thinking ___________ changing her job.

2 Complete the table.

Nouns	**Adjectives**
aggression	*aggressive*
assertiveness	
	emotional
grudge	
	healthy
	hostile
	influential
sense	
suitability	
unwillingness	

3 Which of the adjectives in Ex 2 have positive meanings?

____

____

4 Complete these sentences with the words in the box.

avoid bully face up to hostility power react tension weakness

1 There was a lot of ___________ between the two groups. Nobody said anything, but it was very unpleasant.
2 Ben needed to ___________ the fact that he would never see Jenny again.
3 His biggest ___________ was that he didn't have much influence with his friends.
4 Alice persuaded Tim not to ___________ violently even though Steve had kicked him.
5 Nathan tried to make the peace, but he found a lot of ___________ from the local community.
6 I'm not sure it's always a good idea to ___________ arguments. Sometimes they need to happen.
7 If I were you, I'd never let anyone ___________ you. You need to stop them straight away.
8 The king had an enormous amount of ___________, but he wasn't a good leader.

5 Choose the correct alternative.

1 Gareth had a *smart* / *daft idea*. He suggested that we went for a swim in the middle of the night.
2 Emily decided to *stick with* / *separate from* her boyfriend despite their argument.
3 When Jack arrived home, he was *delighted* / *startled* to see that a letter from his mother-in-law had arrived.
4 Chloe felt a *grudging* / *total* respect for the police officer. She wanted to thank him, but she felt that some of his methods were unprofessional.
5 Ellie and Joshua are both *annoyed* / *influenced* by TV celebrities. They copy their taste in fashion and music.
6 Molly carefully *placed* / *slapped* the poster on her bedroom wall.

Grammar reference

Unit 1

Past simple and present perfect

Past simple

Form (regular verbs)

I You He She It We They	wanted	to escape

I You He She It We They	didn't	want	to escape

Did	I you he she it we they	want	to escape?

Use

You use the past simple to talk about completed times in the past. This period of time is either directly referred to:
Did you enjoy family holidays ***when you were fifteen?***
or is obvious:
Jackie never played with dolls (when she was a child).

Present perfect

Form

You form the present perfect with the verb *have* and the past participle of the main verb.

I You We They	have	lived	in Paris for two years.
He She It	has		

Negative statement: *Martin* ***hasn't heard*** *from Patricia for ages.*
Question: *How long* ***have you known*** *your partner?*

Use

You can use the present perfect to talk about the past and the time up to now.

*Richard****'s made*** *a lot of new friends* ***since he started*** *his English course.* (He started his course some time ago. He met lots of people. They became his friends. He continues to meet new people and make friends.)

Time words and phrases

Time words and phrases help tell us about when something happened or is happening. You use some time words and phrases with the past simple and others with the present perfect.

Normally used with the past simple: *when I was, last year, ago*

Normally used with the present perfect: *ever, just, since*

Used with the past simple or the present perfect: *always, never, for*

David ***changed*** *his job* ***last year.***
*Emma****'s just arrived.***
Robert ***studied*** *medicine* ***for*** *three years.*

Unit 2

Degrees of politeness and formality

There are a number of ways of making requests more polite or formal in English:

1 Use past tense verb forms.

__Can__ you shut the door, please? → *__Could__ you shut the door, please?*

__Will__ you tidy your room, please? → *__Would__ you tidy your room, please?*

2 Use introductory phrases. This changes the word order in the request.

***I'd be very grateful if** you'd turn the radio off.*

***Is it alright if** I close the window?*

***Would you mind if** I leave early today?*

You can also use introductory phrases to apologise or explain something.

***I'm sorry but** Mrs Blackwell's not here today.*

***I'm afraid that** I won't be able to come on Saturday.*

***I apologise for** arriving so late.*

***Well, actually** I forgot to tell Mark about the meeting.*

In the most polite and most formal requests you use past tense forms and introductory phrases. But if you are too polite or formal with your friends they may think you are being unfriendly or insincere.

***I was wondering if** you **would** do me a favour.*

***Do you think** you **could** be a bit quieter, please?*

Unit 3

Giving advice

There are a number of ways to give advice.

Could + infinitive
*You **could** try phoning her.*

Should + infinitive
*You **should** go on a long trip.*

If I were you I'd + infinitive
***If I were you I'd complain** to the manager.*

You might think about + *-ing* form
***You might think about having** a romantic weekend away.*

You use *could*, *If I were you*, and *You might think about* when you want to be polite or formal. You can use *should* to be more direct, or to give stronger advice.

Unit 4

Verb + preposition

Many verbs are followed by a preposition:

*hear of: Have you **heard of** Girls Aloud?*

*read about: **I read about** the fight between the two families.*

*speak to: Corinne won't **speak to** Daniel.*

Most verbs can have more than one preposition. Usually this changes the meaning:

*apologise for: **I apologise for** my behaviour last night.*

*apologise to: I **apologised to** Steven for swearing at his sister.*

*complain about: Leigh **complained about** the food.*

*complain to: Leigh **complained to** the waiter.*

Sometimes using a different preposition after a verb doesn't change the meaning:

speak to / speak with:
*I need to **speak to** / **with** you.*

think about / of:
*I'm **thinking of** / **about** you.*

Sometimes using the same preposition after a verb can have more than one meaning:

*She **went through** the park.* (go through = to cross)

*She **went through** the details.* (go through = to explain)

Wordlist

*** the 2,500 most common English words, ** very common words, * fairly common words

Unit 1
affect *v* /əˈfekt/ ***
affectionate *adj* /əˈfekʃnət/
ambitious *adj* /æmˈbɪʃəs/ **
annoyed *adj* /əˈnɔɪd/ **
approach *n* /əˈprəʊtʃ/ ***
arrogant *adj* /ˈærəgənt/ **
astonishing *adj* /əˈstɒnɪʃɪŋ/ *
background *n* /ˈbækˌgraʊnd/ ***
bad-tempered *adj* /ˌbædˈtempəd/ *
behave *v* /bɪˈheɪv/ **
behaviour *n* /bɪˈheɪvjə/ ***
birth order *n* /ˈbɜːθ ˌɔːdə/
break the rules *phrase* /ˌbreɪk ðə ˈruːlz/
cautious *adj* /ˈkɔːʃəs/ *
characteristic *n* /ˌkærɪktəˈrɪstɪk/ **
claim *v* /kleɪm/ ***
confident *adj* /ˈkɒnfɪd(ə)nt/ **
conform *v* /kənˈfɔːm/ *
conventional *adj* /kənˈvenʃn(ə)l/ ***
cross *adj* /krɒs/
fire (someone) *v* /faɪə (sʌmwʌn)/ ***
generous *adj* /ˈdʒenərəs/ **
hard-working *adj* /ˌhɑːdˈwɜːkɪŋ/ *
high-achiever *n* /ˌhaɪəˈtʃiːvə/
independent *adj* /ˌɪndɪˈpendənt/ ***
influence *n* /ˈɪnfluəns/ ***
insensitive *adj* /ɪnˈsensətɪv/
leave (someone) out *v* /ˌliːv (sʌmwʌn) ˈaʊt/
mature *adj* /məˈtʃʊə/ **
narrow-minded *adj* /ˌnærəʊˈmaɪndɪd/
negotiate *v* /nɪˈgəʊʃieɪt/ **
obedient *adj* /əˈbiːdiənt/ *
opposites *n* /ˈɒpəzɪts/ *
personality *n* /pɜːsəˈnæləti/ ***
promote *v* /prəˈməʊt/ ***
proposal *n* /prəˈpəʊzl/ ***
psychologist *n* /saɪˈkɒlədʒɪst/ **
radical *adj* /ˈrædɪkl/ *
reach an agreement *phrase*
/ˌriːtʃ ən əˈgriːmənt/
rebel *n* /ˈrebl/ **
rebellious *adj* /rɪˈbeljəs/
reliable *adj* /rɪˈlaɪəbl/ **
responsible *adj* /rɪˈspɒnsəbl/ ***
risk-taking *adj* /ˈrɪskˌteɪkɪŋ/
selfish *adj* /ˈselfɪʃ/ *
self-motivated *adj* /ˌselfˈməʊtɪˌveɪtɪd/
sociable *adj* /ˈsəʊʃəbl/
status-conscious *adj* /ˈsteɪtəsˌkɒnʃəs/
strict *adj* /strɪkt/ **
successful *adj* /səkˈsesfl/ ***
unselfish *adj* /ʌnˈselfɪʃ/

Unit 2
amazing *ad* /əˈmeɪzɪŋ/ **
antisocial *adj* /ˌæntiˈsəʊʃl/
appointment *n* /əˈpɔɪntmənt/ ***
assume *v* /əˈsjuːm/ ***
avoid *v* /əˈvɔɪd/ ***
boast *v* /bəʊst/ *
bossy *adj* /ˈbɒsi/
buyer *n* /ˈbaɪə/ ***
campaign *n* /kæmˈpeɪn/ ***
clear up *v* /ˌklɪə ˈʌp/
compensation *n* /ˌkɒmpənˈseɪʃn/ **
complain *v* / complaint *n*
/kəmˈpleɪn/ /kəmˈpleɪnt/
convict *v* / conviction *n*
/kənˈvɪkt/ /kənˈvɪkʃn/ **
court *n* /kɔːt/ ***
defrost *v* /diːˈfrɒst/
depress *v* /dɪˈpres/ *
dishes *n* /ˈdɪʃɪz/ **
dispute *n* /dɪsˈpjuːt/ ***
embarrassing *adj* /ɪmˈbærəsɪŋ/ *
exaggerate *v* /ɪgˈzædʒəˌreɪt/ *
fair share *n* /ˌfeə ˈʃeə/
forgetful *adj* /fəˈgetfl/
fridge *n* /frɪdʒ/ *
harassment *n* /ˈhærəsmənt/ *
hoover *v* /ˈhuːvə/
housemate *n* /ˈhaʊsˌmeɪt/
housework *n* /ˈhaʊsˌwɜːk/ *
inform *v* /ɪnˈfɔːm/ ***
insult *n* / insulting *adj* /ˈɪnsʌlt/ /ɪnˈsʌltɪŋ/ *
lawyer *n* /ˈlɔːjə/ ***
mess *n* /mes/ **
obscene *adj* /əbˈsiːn/
obsessed *adj* /əbˈsest/ *
potential *adj* /pəˈtenʃl/ ***
probation *n* /prəˈbeɪʃn/ *
quality *n* /ˈkwɒləti/ ***
resolve *v* /rɪˈzɒlv/ *
rubbish *n* /ˈrʌbɪʃ/ **
sense of humour *n* /ˌsens əv ˈhjuːmə/
share *n* /ʃeə/ ***
sink *n* /sɪŋk/
slob *n* /slɒb/
stranger *n* /ˈstreɪndʒə/ **
sue *v* /suː/ **
swear *v* /sweə/ **
switch on /off *v* /ˌswɪtʃ ˈɒn/ˈɒf/
tidy up *v* /ˌtaɪdi ˈʌp/
unpleasant *adj* /ʌnˈpleznt/ **
unreasonable *adj* /ʌnˈriːznəbl/ *
unreliable *adj* /ˌʌnrɪˈlaɪəbl/ *
untidy *adj* /ʌnˈtaɪdi/ *
wash up *v* /ˌwɒʃ ˈʌp/

Unit 3
advice *n* /advise *v* /ədˈvaɪs/ /ədˈvaɪz/ ***
afford *v* /əˈfɔːd/ ***
approve *v* /əˈpruːv/ ***
awkward *adj* /ˈɔːkwəd/ **
break up *v* /ˌbreɪk ˈʌp/
catch up *v* /ˌkætʃ ˈʌp/
contribute *v* /kənˈtrɪbjuːt/ ***
couple *n* /ˈkʌpl/ ***
deal with *v* /ˈdiːl ˌwɪð/
debt *n* /det/ ***
dilemma *n* /dɪˈlemə/ ***
equality *n* / equally *adv*
/ɪˈkwɒləti/ /ˈiːkwəli/ **
escape *v* /ɪˈskeɪp/ ***
fall out *v* /ˌfɔːl ˈaʊt/
feel guilty *phrase* /ˌfiːl ˈgɪlti/
forgive *v* /fəˈgɪv/ **
get away *v* /ˌget əˈweɪ/
get on *v* /ˌget ˈɒn/
get together *v* /ˌget təˈgeðə/
go away *v* /ˌgəʊ əˈweɪ/
go out *v* /ˌgəʊ ˈaʊt/
hit it off *v* /ˌhɪt ɪt ˈɒf/
house husband *n* /ˈhaʊs ˌhʌzbənd/
ideal *adj* /aɪˈdɪəl/ **
insist *v* /ɪnˈsɪst/ ***
invent *v* /ɪnˈvent/ **
joint *adj* /dʒɔɪnt/ ***
law *n* /lɔː/ ***
let down *v* /ˌlet ˈdaʊn/
living expenses *n* /ˈlɪvɪŋ ɪkˌspensɪz/
lose weight *phrase* /ˌluːz ˈweɪt/
nanny *n* /ˈnæni/
partner *n* /ˈpɑːtnə/ ***
part-time *adj* /ˌpɑːtˈtaɪm/
pay off *v* /ˌpeɪ ˈɒf/
pretend *v* /prɪˈtend/ **
push (someone) into (something) *v*
/pʊʃ (sʌmwʌn) ɪntə (sʌmθɪŋ)/
refuse *v* /rɪˈfjuːz/ ***
request *n* /rɪˈkwest/ ***
salary *n* /ˈsæləri/ **
save (money) *v* /seɪv (mʌni)/ ***
shocked *adj* /ʃɒkt/ *
solve *v* /sɒlv/ ***
take over *v* /ˌteɪk ˈəʊvə/

Unit 4
aggressive *adj* /əˈgresɪv/ **
agreement *n* /əˈgriːmənt/ ***
apologise *v* /əˈpɒlədʒaɪz/ **
assertive *adj* /əˈsɜːtɪv/
attack v /əˈtæk/ ***
avoid *v* /əˈvɔɪd/ ***
bully *v* /ˈbʊli/ *
catholic nationalist *n* /ˌkæθlɪk ˈnæʃnəlɪst/
civil war *n* /ˈsɪvl wɔː/ *
commit *v* /kəˈmɪt/ ***
community *n* /kəˈmjuːnəti/ ***
conflict *n* /ˈkɒnflɪkt/ ***
controversial *adj* /ˌkɒntrəˈvɜːʃl/ **
daft *adj* /dɑːft/ *
defeat *v* /dɪˈfiːt/ **
dominate *v* /ˈdɒmɪˌneɪt/ **
economic growth *n* /ˌiːkəˌnɒmɪk ˈgrəʊθ/
emigrate *v* /ˈemɪgreɪt/
emotion *n* /ɪˈməʊʃn/ ***
face up to *v* /ˌfeɪs ˈʌp tuː/
famine *n* /ˈfæmɪn/ *
growl *v* /graʊl/ *
grudging *adj* /ˈgrʌdʒɪŋ/
hostility *n* /hɒˈstɪləti/ **
human relations *n* /ˌhjuːmən rɪˈleɪʃnz/
influence *n* /ˈɪnfluəns/ ***
keep the peace *v* /ˌkiːp ðə ˈpiːs/
kill *v* /kɪl/ ***
make up *v* /ˌmeɪk ˈʌp/
mental health *n* /ˌmentl ˈhelθ/
mission *n* /ˈmɪʃn/ **
passive *adj* /ˈpæsɪv/ **
persuade *v* /pəˈsweɪd/ ***
point of view *n* /ˌpɔɪnt əv ˈvjuː/ **
political rights *n* /pəˌlɪtɪkl ˈraɪts/
poverty *n* /ˈpɒvəti/ **
power *n* /ˈpaʊə/ ***
protest *v* /prəˈtest/ **
protestant unionist *n* /ˌprɒtɪstənt ˈjuːnjənɪst/
react *v* /riˈækt/ **
sensible *adj* /ˈsensəbl/ **
separate *v* /ˈsepəˌreɪt/ ***
set a trend *phrase* /ˌset ə ˈtrend/
set an example *phrase* /ˌset ən ɪgˈzɑːmpl/
share *v* /ʃeə/ ***
slap on *v* /ˌslæp ˈɒn/
specialist *n* /ˈspeʃəlɪst/ **
startled *adj* /ˈstɑːtld/ *
stay on good terms *phrase*
/ˌsteɪ ɒn ˌgʊd ˈtɜːmz/
stick out your tongue *phrase*
/ˌstɪk aʊt jə ˈtʌŋ/
stick with *v* /ˈstɪk ˌwɪð/
stupid *adj* /ˈstjuːpɪd/ **
suitable *adj* /ˈsuːtəbl/ ***
superior *adj* /suːˈpɪəriə/ **
take sides *v* /ˌteɪk ˈsaɪdz/
tension *n* /ˈtenʃn/ ***
unwilling *adj* /ʌnˈwɪlɪŋ/ *
up to something *phrase* /ʌp tə sʌmθɪŋ/
upset *adj* /ʌpˈset/ **
viewpoint *n* /ˈvjuːpɔɪnt/ *
violence *n* /ˈvaɪələns/ ***
waste time *v* /ˌweɪst ˈtaɪm/
weakness *n* /ˈwiːknəs/ **

Communication activities

Student A

Unit 2, Pronunciation and speaking Ex 5 page 41

You have recently moved into a shared house with student B. You do not know each other very well and after two months there are some things that you need to discuss. Talk to student B about the things you would like to change in the house. You must include as many of these sentences as possible in your conversation.

1 Do you mind if I sing in the shower?
2 That smelly cheese you really love makes me feel sick.
3 I'm happy to wash your socks if you make me breakfast every morning.
4 Did I tell you that I sleepwalk?
5 I think I saw a rat in your room the other day.
6 Could you stop eating my oranges?

Act out your conversation to the rest of the class.

Listening scripts

Unit 1 Family ties

Listening script 14

Reading text from page 35

Listening script 15

(Amanda)
People closest to me? Well the two people that I'm closest to are my mum, and my boyfriend, Nick. Mum and I have been through some difficult times, especially when I was about 14 to 15, but now that I don't live at home any more we get on much better. I always talk things through with her. I met Nick about a year ago. He's a very affectionate and generous person, and he's also really good fun to be with. The only thing is that I don't see him as often as I want to because he lives about an hour away from me. I spend a lot of time with my friend, Kerri. We see each other at least twice a week. We've known each other since we were 10 and totally share the same sense of humour. She's one of those people that are always cheerful and look on the bright side of life. I used to be quite close to a boy called Adam, who I met at university, but about six months ago he met his girlfriend and now he ignores his old friends and spends all his time with her. When we go out together he tries to phone his girlfriend every five minutes, which is really irritating.
My family? Well I've got two sisters, but the age gap between us is so big that I'm not really close to either of them. I see Helen about once every six months, but Laura's very selfish. She only cares about herself and her career. She didn't even call me when I broke my leg and was in hospital for a week! How insensitive is that?

Unit 2 Neighbours

Listening script 16

(NR = Newsreader; Mrs T = Mrs Thomas)

NR: ... the hospital which cost £100 million pounds was opened two months ahead of schedule.
A Brighton couple are considering suing their neighbour for reducing the value of their home by £50,000. Robert and Annabel Thomas are unable to sell their £200,000 three-bedroom house as a result of a 5-year campaign of hate by their neighbour, Dennis Rogers.

Mrs T: One day, Mr Rogers suddenly became obsessed with making our lives a living nightmare. From then on it hasn't stopped. Every day there is something. He throws bits of old rubbish into our garden and shouts and swears at us and our visitors – it's so embarrassing ... and frightening.

NR: The problem began when Mr Rogers became annoyed with the Thomases over a party they held five years ago. Apparently Mr Rogers became angry because guests parked cars in front of his house and he claimed that loud music went on until 3 o'clock in the morning. The Thomases say that they had informed all their neighbours in advance of their party and that no-one complained at the time. They say that since then Mr Rogers has shouted insults over the fence and thrown old beds, chairs, bicycles, and bits of wood into their garden. They also claim that every summer he has continuously sung the song 'Happy Hippo' whenever he sees Mrs Thomas sunbathing in the garden. In December, the Thomases took Mr Rogers to court and he was convicted of harassment. Mr Rogers had to pay compensation of £1,000 and was given 18 months probation. The Thomases have now decided they want to move away from their neighbour from hell. However, there is a problem. Legally house sellers have to inform potential buyers of any disputes with neighbours and the Thomases have been warned by their estate agent that the conflict has decreased the value of their house by £50,000. According to Mr and Mrs Thomas several potential buyers have lost interest after being told about Mr Rogers.

Mrs T: Who would want to live next to someone like Mr Rogers? I don't think he's normal. He needs treatment. You never know what he's going to do next. If we lose money on the sale of our house we will definitely sue Mr Rogers. We've suffered enough. Why should we have to pay for his unreasonable behaviour?

NR: And now the weather: After a chilly start, there will be sunny intervals ...

Listening script 17

Reading text from page 40

Listening script 18

Pronunciation and speaking Ex 1 page 41

Listening script 19

Pronunciation and speaking Ex 2 page 41

Unit 3 Partners

Listening script 20

Reading text from page 42

Listening script 21

(AD = Arabella Doyle; J = Jane)

AD: Welcome to today's Dr Arabella Doyle Show. I'm Arabella Doyle and I'm here to help ordinary people with everyday problems. Our first caller is Jane on line 1. Hello, Jane.

J: Hello Dr Doyle. I'd just like to say that I'm a great fan of your show. I think it's wonderful how you help people.

AD: Thanks for that Jane. Now, what's your problem?

J: Well, my problem is this. My husband feels less of a man because I earn more than him and pay for everything.

AD: I see and do you resent having to pay for everything?

J: Oh no, I'm not complaining about him. That's not the case at all – I'm perfectly happy to do it. I don't mind that he doesn't contribute, but he feels awkward about it.

AD: How do you deal with this situation?

J: Well, if we're having a meal in a restaurant with friends, I sometimes pass him money under the table so that he can be seen to pay in public. Other times I pretend to win cash prizes so that we can go on holiday without him feeling guilty.

AD: Do you have children?

J: Yes, we've two children under five.

AD: So, does your husband stay at home to look after them?

J: No, he works. But his salary is very low.

AD: So, he isn't a house husband.

J: No we have a full-time nanny. I've often wondered if he'd feel better being a house husband, but I'm not at all sure that it's the right thing to suggest.

AD: Hmm, Jane, if your husband wanted to be at home all day with the kids, he'd offer. You shouldn't push him into being a house husband.

J: I see. What would you do, if you were me?

AD: Well Jane, the truth is that if I were you I'd probably do what you're doing. You know, although most men have accepted aspects of equality with women, many still make an exception when it comes to money matters. The rule seems to be that your salary is a wonderful thing to be celebrated and enjoyed, as long as you don't earn more than he does.

J: That doesn't make dealing with my problems any easier, though!

AD: True, but you might think about giving your husband money before you go out rather than in the restaurant. That would make it easier. Or you could open a joint bank account for his salary and either all or part of yours. What do you think about that?

J: Well it's certainly something to consider. Thank you so much for your advice.

AD: Thank you Jane and good luck. Now for our next caller ...

Unit 4 Troubles

Listening script 22

Reading text from page 47

Listening script 23

(Specialist)
Obviously conflict is an important part of human relations, it's something we can't avoid when we have dealings with other people. Other people inevitably do things that upset us, or say things that we disagree with. So it's not a question of avoiding conflict; it's how we deal with it that's important for our long term mental health.
There are basically three reactions. Firstly you can do nothing. This is what I call the 'passive' response. This may sometimes be a good idea, for example if you're faced with a difficult or violent person. Doing nothing may help him or her to calm down. But there are lots of disadvantages if you always avoid conflict, too. You are saying 'my opinion is not worth anything' and some people will take advantage of what they see as your weakness.
The second reaction to conflict is the complete opposite. This is what I call the 'aggressive' response. It's what happens when you can't control your emotions, and you begin to shout at people or dominate them in

other ways. It's useful in emergencies, or when you need to give orders, but most of the time it's just unkind or selfish. Most people don't like being bullied, and you will end up losing your friends if you are not careful.
The third reaction to conflict is to face up to it and put forward your own views. It's called the 'assertive' response. If you have a viewpoint, and you feel strongly about what someone has done, you have the right to let the other person know how you feel, and so has the other person. If you and the other person can both walk away from the discussion feeling that you have put forward your points of view and listened to the other person's views, then you will both feel good about it, and there won't be bad feelings between you. I can't think of any disadvantages to the assertive response.

Unit 5 Review

Listening script 24

(I = Interviewer; T = Tony; J = Jacquie)
I: Tony, can you remember when you first met Jacquie?
T: 1981.
I: 1981. Oh! You remember!
T: Yes.
I: And, where were you?
T: In north London.
I: What was going on?
T: It was a meeting of the local conservation society.
I: And were you both at the meeting?
T: Actually, it was more of a party than a meeting. But, yes, we were both there.
I: I see. And were you introduced to Jacquie?
T: Not quite. Erm ... I was one of the guest speakers. And I did my little speech, but she kept interrupting me, shouting out from the back of the room!
I: Can you remember what she was wearing?
T: No.
I: You can't?
T: Not at all.
I: Okay.
T: Though it might have been blue.
I: Oh it might have been blue? So, anyway, what were your first impressions?
T: Oh! I was over the moon. I thought she was wonderful!
I: So immediately, you fell for her.
T: Oh yes! Absolutely. Immediately.
I: And did you ask her out?
T: No, I think I asked if I could take her home.
I: Yes?
T: To which she replied 'Yes, but I've got my friend with me.' So I ended up taking her and her friend home.
I: Okay. And then you got her phone number, and ...
T: Yes, I can't quite remember how it happened after that. I must have got her phone number.
I: So after that you got in touch with her and then you went on a date?
T: Yes, but I can't remember where we went.
I: Alright. Well, I think I'm going to ask Jacquie what she remembers.
T: That could be interesting!
I: Jacquie I've been talking to Tony about how you met. Can you remember when that was?
J: It was autumn 1982.
I: And where were you?
J: I'd gone with a friend to a little gathering of the Historical Society. It was near where we lived.
I: And Tony was there too?
J: Yes. It was supposed to be a party but then this man, Tony, started to give a speech.
I: About architecture?
J: Oh something like that. Anyway it just went on and on and he had to be stopped, so I started to ask him some questions.
I: And what happened then?
J: Well I think erm ... when he eventually finished the speech he came up to me and erm ... we were chatting.
I: Can you remember what he was wearing?
J: Oh good heavens! Erm ... I'm pretty sure it was jeans and a denim jacket. I can remember the shirt, too. It was a horrible shiny orange thing.
I: And what did you think?
J: Well, he was fun and lively, but maybe a bit too full of himself, you know, bit arrogant.
I: What happened after the party?
J: Well I do remember I was with my friend Stella and Tony came home with us. I think he kissed me good night. That was nice!
I: Did you go out on a date after that?
J: Well, yes, the next evening in fact. We went out to dinner.
I: And that was that!
J: That was that!

Listening script 25

Song from page 52

Communication activities

Student B

Unit 2, Pronunciation and speaking Ex 5 page 41

You have recently moved into a shared house with student A. You do not know each other very well and after two months there are some things that you need to discuss. Talk to student A about the things you would like to change in the house. You must include as many of these sentences as possible in your conversation.

1 Have I told you about my rat?
2 Could you stop using my shampoo to wash your socks?
3 Did I see you sleepwalking last night?
4 Do you mind if I dance hip hop in my room?
5 What is that strange meat you have in the fridge?
6 My grandmother will be moving in with us next week.

Act out your conversation to the rest of the class.

Module 3
Time out

Unit	Topic	Language study	Vocabulary	Main skills
1 **Crossing the line** pages 66–69	• Beckham 1, Ferguson 1 (Managing anger) • Famous olympic moments	• Describing past events (past simple, past continuous, past perfect)	• Discussing sport • Sports events	• **Reading:** ordering events • **Speaking:** responding to a text; presenting an argument • **Listening:** identifying key information • **Writing:** an opinion letter
2 **Is it art?** pages 70–73	• Basher (Modern art) • Describing art	• Qualifying adjectives: (*very*, *absolutely* and *quite*)	• Colours and shades	• **Listening:** checking information • **Reading:** understanding opinions • **Speaking:** expressing opinions about art • **Pronunciation:** giving opinions using intonation
3 **Fashion victims** pages 74–77	• Hey, she's wearing my clothes! (Interview with a designer) • Confessions of a shopaholic	• Linking ideas • The order of adjectives	• Clothes (pattern, material, style)	• **Reading:** understanding main information in a text • **Speaking:** discussing clothes and fashion; comparing responses to a survey • **Listening:** extracting details from an interview
4 **Globetrotting** pages 78–81	• Off the beaten track with David Abram (Travel writing) • Nightmare journeys	• Verb + infinitive or *-ing*	• Phrasal verbs: travel • Means of transport	• **Reading:** identifying particular information • **Listening:** understanding key references • **Speaking:** telling a story about a nightmare journey • **Writing:** a review about a place

• **Use CD2 for listening activities in this module**

1 Crossing the line

LEARNING AIMS

- Can describe past events
- Can use sports vocabulary and discuss sport
- Can present an argument

Lead-in

1 Discuss your feelings about sport. Use these questions to help you.

1 Do you enjoy watching or playing sport? Which sports?
2 Would you like to be a professional sports player? Why? / Why not?
3 What problems are there in the world of sport today?

Reading

1 Look at the photos on page 67. What do you know about David Beckham and his private life? Why do you think he has become a superstar? What's Alex Ferguson's job?

2 **01** Read the text on page 67 and put the events in the correct order.

a Alex Ferguson criticised Beckham ☐
b An Arsenal player scored a goal ☐
c Alex Ferguson kicked a boot at Beckham ☐
d Beckham walked past Ferguson in the lounge ☐
e Beckham attacked Ferguson ☐
f Ferguson apologised ☐

3 Match these words from the text to the definitions.

1	bloke	a	attack someone
2	own up	b	say bad words
3	calm down	c	man
4	swear	d	feeling of great anger
5	go for	e	admit your mistake
6	rage	f	return to normal after a period of anger

4 Work with a partner and discuss these questions.

1 Who do you think behaved worse in this incident, David Beckham or Alex Ferguson?

2 In which of the following circumstances are you most likely to lose your temper?
- Being accused of something you didn't do
- Being kept waiting by a friend or partner
- Seeing someone being cruel to a child or an animal
- Arguing with an official who won't back down or change their mind about something
- Being stuck in a traffic jam

3 Have you lost your temper in the past year? What about? How did you react? Is it OK to lose your temper occasionally?

Beckham 1, Ferguson 1

We trooped back into the dressing room afterwards. I took my boots and shin pads off straight away because I'd got a kick on my leg. The boss came in, shut the door, took his jacket off and hung it up on a hook. His first words were:

'David. What about the second goal? What were you doing?'

Was he blaming me? I was taken completely by surprise.

'It wasn't my fault. Their **blokes** made a run off someone in central midfield.'

The boss kept going: 'We told you about it before the game. The problem with you is you don't let anyone talk to you. You don't listen.'

I couldn't believe it. I'd been listening – and wanting to listen – my whole career. I'd listened to the boss since the first day we'd met and I was listening now.

'David. When you're wrong, you've got to **own up**.'

'Boss I'm sorry. I'm not wrong here. This wasn't my fault and I'm not taking the blame for it.'

'No. Take the blame is what you're going to do.'

Everybody else in the dressing room could hear what was going on. Surely, everybody else knew I was right: you could have pointed your finger at half a dozen of the team in the build-up to Arsenal's second goal. But it was all my fault according to the boss. I felt like I was being bullied, and I **swore** at him; something no player, certainly no United player, should ever do to the manager.

The boss took a step or two towards me from the other side of the room. There was a boot on the floor. He swung his leg and kicked it. At me? At the wall? It could have been anywhere, he was that angry now. I felt a sharp pain just over my left eye where the boot had hit me. I put one hand up to it and found myself wiping blood away off my eyebrow. I **went for** the boss. I don't know if I've ever lost control like that in my life before. A couple of lads stood up. I was grabbed by Giggsy* first, then by Gary** and Ruud van Nistelrooy. Suddenly it was like some mad scene out of a gangster movie, with them holding me back as I tried to get to the boss. He stepped back, I think quite shocked at what had happened. Probably a minute at most was how long the real **rage** lasted. I **calmed down** a bit and went through into the treatment room. When I came back the boss was there.

'I'm sorry David. I didn't mean to do that.'

I couldn't even bring myself to look at him. I didn't say anything, just walked straight past and through into the players' lounge. Victoria was there. I wanted to get out of Old Trafford*** and home.

* Ryan Giggs ** Gary Neville
*** Manchester United's football stadium

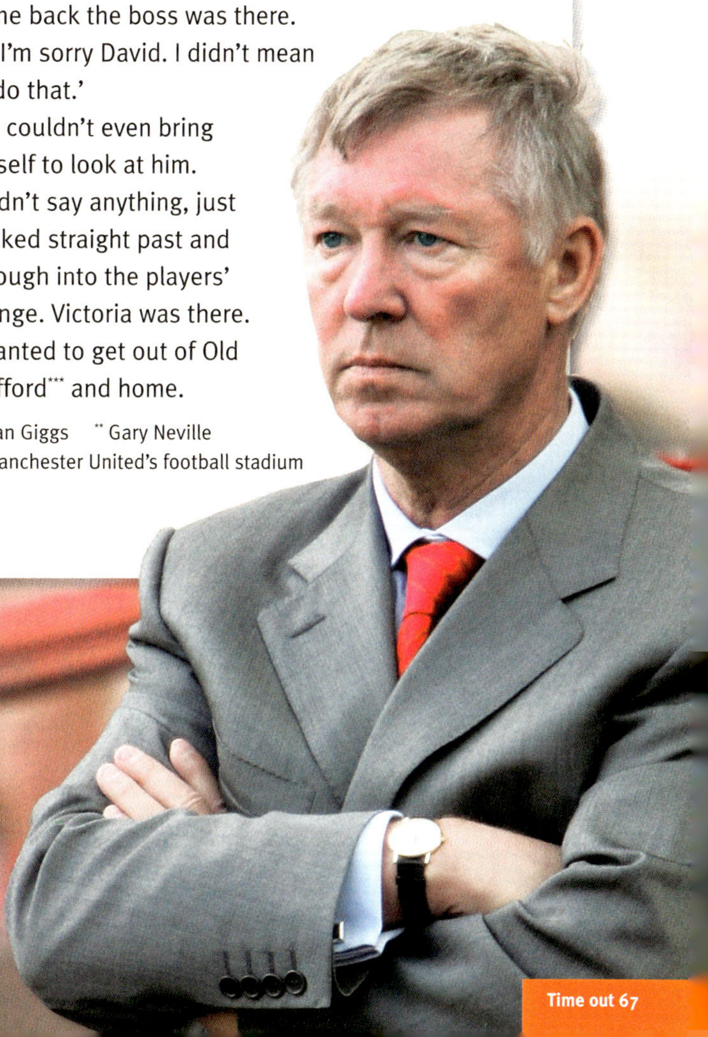

Source: *David Beckham: My Side* by David Beckham with Tom Watt, published by Collins Willow 2003

LANGUAGE STUDY

Describing past events

1 Look at the examples and complete the table. Use *past simple*, *past perfect* and *past continuous*.

Past tenses

Example	Use	Form
*They **were holding** me **back** as I tried to get to the boss*	What was happening at the time another event took place	______________
*The boss **came in** and **shut** the door*	One past event after another, described in order	______________
*I felt a pain over my left eye where the boot **had hit** me*	Describing an event that happened earlier in the past	______________

2 Compare these sentences. Explain the differences in meaning.

a *When Alex got to the dressing room, David was taking off his boots.*
b *When Alex got to the dressing room, David took off his boots.*
c *When Alex got to the dressing room, David had taken off his boots.*

Grammar reference page 90

3 Complete the story with the correct form of the verbs.

I support Burnley football club. I used to go and see them every week. One Saturday, my friend Alan and I went to watch a cup match with a club from a higher division. Burnley (1 play) ____________ really well, and they won. As we (2 walk) ____________ back to the car I (3 see) ____________ three blokes. They (4 wear) ____________ shirts from the other club. They (5 come) ____________ up to me. Alan wasn't with me because we (6 become) ____________ separated in the crowd. The blokes (7 start) ____________ to beat me up. They (8 hit) ____________ me and (9 kick) ____________ me. I (10 see) ____________ Alan a short distance from me and I (11 shout) ____________ for help. He could see what (12 happen) ____________ but he (13 not come) ____________ and help me. Instead he (14 run away) ____________ . I don't go to matches anymore.

4 Work with a partner and discuss these questions.

1 Have you ever seen a violent incident? What happened?
2 Have you ever been let down by a friend, or let down a friend yourself?

Great Olympic moments

Vocabulary and listening

1 Guess what these Olympic symbols represent. Write the name of the sport next to the symbol.

1 l______ j______ 2 b______ 3 j______ 4 r______ 5 s______ 6 g______ 7 r______

2 02 Listen to Jenny, Ben and Sarah discussing famous Olympic moments. In which events were these athletes famous?

	Athlete	**Event**
1	Steve Redgrave	______________
2	Nadia Comaneci	______________
3	Dorando Pietri	______________
4	Carl Lewis	______________
5	Ben Johnson	______________

3 Listen again and answer these questions.

1 Where did Steve Redgrave win his fifth gold medal?
2 Why didn't Dorando Pietri win an Olympic medal?
3 Why does Jenny think Nadia Comaneci shouldn't have been competing at the Olympic Games?
4 Why didn't Ben Johnson win a gold medal?
5 Which athletes are in this photo? What were they doing?

Speaking

1 Work in groups. You are going to represent **one** of these organisations. Prepare arguments for a five-minute presentation to the class.

- **Olympic Fan Club:** You are a group of very enthusiastic Olympic supporters and you'd like the games to be held every two years, instead of four.
- **Anti-Boxing Organisation:** You are a group which believes that boxing is a dangerous sport that should be withdrawn from the Olympics.
- **Golf Society:** You are a group of professional golf players who feel that golf should be added to the Olympics.
- **Children's Welfare Society:** You are a group of adults who believe that teenagers under the age of 16 should not be allowed to participate in the Olympics.

2 Imagine your class is the Olympic Advisory Committee. Listen to each presentation, then ask questions and discuss the ideas that have been presented. Vote to decide if the group's arguments are accepted or not.

Writing

1 Write a letter to the Olympic Advisory Committee expressing your views about the decisions that they reached in Speaking Ex 2. Give reasons for your views. Use these phrases to help you.

Firstly, concerning the timetable of the Games …
As far as boxing is concerned …
Regarding golf …
We discussed the age rule and …

CD-ROM For more activities go to **Time out Unit 1**

2 Is it art?

LEARNING AIMS

- Can qualify adjectives
- Can express opinions about art
- Can give opinions using intonation

Lead-in

1 Look at the pictures and find examples of a painting, a sketch, a sculpture, graffiti, and pottery. What other types of art do you know?

2 Work with a partner. What objects do you have in your house that you think of as artwork? Say which ones you like and which you dislike.

Basher

Listening

1 Match these words to the definitions.

commercial	contemporary	distinctive
emotional	flexible	

1 different from other things _______________
2 modern _______________
3 related to business or making money _______________
4 able to make changes _______________
5 expressing strong feelings _______________

2 03 Listen to the first part of the interview with Basher and put the events in the correct order.

a He played in a band. ☐
b He became an independent artist. ☐
c He worked as an illustrator. ☐
d He went to university. ☐
e He managed some pop bands and record producers. ☐

3 04 Listen to the whole interview and choose the correct alternative.

1 He worked as an illustrator for *several years* / *one year*.
2 He *didn't enjoy* / *enjoyed* managing pop bands and record producers.
3 The first time he tried to sell his art at Spitalfields Market he *was* / *wasn't* very successful.
4 He *produces* / *has been influenced by* graffiti and comics.
5 He *uses* / *doesn't use* computer programs to create images.
6 Basher *is* / *isn't* flexible about how his work is used.

4 Work with a partner and discuss these questions.

1 Would you buy Basher's work on a T-shirt or a poster? Why? / Why not?
2 What else could he print his art onto?
3 Do you think it's possible to be a real artist and also a businessman?
4 Do you think Basher is right to think of his art as a way of making money?

LANGUAGE STUDY

Qualifying adjectives

very, *absolutely* and *quite*

1 You can make most adjectives stronger by using *very*.
Example: big → *very* big

But you can't use *very* with all adjectives.
Example: enormous → *absolutely* enormous

What would you use with these adjectives, *very* or *absolutely*?

bad	big	fantastic	good	huge	nice	small	terrible	tiny	wonderful

2 Compare the adjectives in Ex 1. What's the difference between those that use *very* and those that use *absolutely*?

3 Work with a partner. Make a list of ten more adjectives. Would you use *very* or *absolutely* with them? Test another pair of students.

4 Read these sentences and decide what two different meanings of *quite* they show.

1 *This print is quite interesting, but it's not my style.*
2 *This sculpture is quite extraordinary – I love it.*

5 Work with a partner. Use *quite* with the adjectives in Ex 1. With which adjectives does *quite* have meaning 1 in Ex 4? With which adjectives does *quite* have meaning 2?

Grammar reference page 91

6 Complete these sentences with *very*, *absolutely*, or *quite*. Sometimes there is more than one correct answer.

1 The painting is ____________ small but I think it's ____________ good.
2 I like Basher's work. In fact I think it's ____________ fantastic.
3 This photo of me is ____________ terrible. You can only see my feet.
4 The design on that t-shirt is ____________ nice, but I'm not going to buy it.
5 The artist achieved something ____________ amazing. Everyone was impressed by the new statue.

7 Complete these sentences with a suitable adjective.

1 I think modern art is quite ____________.
2 I couldn't even look at the picture. It was quite ____________.
3 My mobile phone is like a work of art. The design is very____________.
4 I had my picture painted, but it was absolutely ____________.

Describing art

Vocabulary

1 Label the painting with the colours in the box.

beige khaki navy purple scarlet turquoise

1 ______________

2 ______________

3 ______________

4 ______________

5 ______________

6 ______________

2 Some colours have different shades. Find examples of these different shades in the painting, and in your classroom.

DARK GREEN	LIGHT GREEN	BRIGHT GREEN	DULL GREEN

1

2

3 Match these descriptions to the artworks on this page. Do you agree with them?

a This is a very interesting picture. It's completely abstract. The use of colour is vibrant and unexpected. The dull grey and brown lines are a marvellous contrast to the bright scarlet background.

b For me this is quite boring. She's in an empty room. Why? What does that say about her? There's no expression on her face. It does nothing for me.

c I adore this. It's made of wood but the shape is really fascinating. It makes me want to touch it and feel the curves. It catches the light in lots of interesting ways.

d I think it's absolutely awful! When you see this kind of thing in an art gallery you are not sure if it's a work of art or if builders have left some materials lying around. It's just a joke, and the artist is laughing at us.

4 Complete the table with the phrases in the box.

For me this is quite boring I adore this It does nothing for me
It makes me want to ... It's absolutely awful It's completely abstract
It's just a joke This is a very interesting picture

Expressing opinions about art

Positive	Neutral	Negative
		It's just a joke

3

5 Work with a partner. One of you is a successful but greedy art dealer, and the other is a wealthy but suspicious customer. The art dealer has four minutes to persuade the customer to buy one of the works of art in Ex 3 and agree on a price.

4

Giving opinions using intonation

Pronunciation

1 **05** Listen to this conversation. Which speaker feels strongly about the artwork? Which speaker doesn't have strong opinions about it?

A: What do you think of this image?

B: It's quite nice.

A: I think it's absolutely fabulous. Look at the colours.

B: Mmm. They're OK. But I prefer something more subtle.

2 Listen again and repeat the conversation. Use the correct intonation.

Reading and listening

1 **06** Read and listen to this extract from a play. Find examples of the intonation patterns in Pronunciation Ex 1.

2 What do Marc and Serge each think about modern art?

Marc: Serge, you haven't bought this painting for two hundred thousand francs?*

Serge: You don't understand. That's what it costs. It's an Antrios.

Marc: You haven't bought this painting for two hundred thousand francs?

Serge: I might have known you'd miss the point.

Marc: You paid two hundred thousand francs for this rubbish?

Serge: What do you mean, 'this rubbish'?

Marc: Serge, where's your sense of humour? Why aren't you laughing? … It's fantastic, you buying this painting.

Serge: I don't care how fantastic you think it is, I don't mind if you laugh, but I would like to know what you mean by 'this rubbish'.

Marc: This is a joke isn't it?

Serge: No, it isn't. By whose standards is it rubbish? If you call something rubbish, you need to have some criterion to judge it by.

Marc: Who are you talking to? Who do you think you're talking to? Hello!

Serge: You have no interest whatsoever in contemporary painting. You never have had. This is a field, about which you know absolutely nothing, so how can you assert that any given object, which conforms to laws you don't understand, is rubbish?

Marc: Because it is. It's rubbish. I'm sorry.

*franc = French money before the Euro
Source: *Art* by Yasmina Reza, translated by Christopher Hampton. Published by Faber and Faber

3 Work with a partner and discuss these questions.

1 Which of the two characters do you agree with?
2 Could you be friends with someone who had very different opinions from you?

4 Work with a partner. Read the extract aloud. Think about your intonation.

Speaking

1 Work with a partner. You are going to prepare a short sales presentation about a piece of artwork for the class. First plan your presentation. Think about:

- Which piece of artwork you are going to describe and which one of you likes / dislikes it. Examples: an object in the classroom, something you have drawn, a famous painting you both know, etc.
- How you are going to describe it: the type of art it is, the colours and shades.
- The language you are going to use to express your opinions about the artwork.

2 Make your sales presentation to the class.

CD-ROM For more activities go to **Time out Unit 2**

3 Fashion victims

LEARNING AIMS

- Can link ideas
- Can use adjectives in the correct order
- Can discuss clothes and fashion

Lead-in

1 What do you think of the clothes the people in the photos are wearing?

2 Work with a partner. Which of these statements do you agree with? Discuss your ideas.

- Your clothes say a lot about your character.
- People who go shopping every week have no other hobbies or interests.
- People choose particular clothes styles so that they can fit into a new group of friends.
- Spending time and money on your appearance doesn't mean that you're vain.

Reading and vocabulary

1 **07** Read the article about Romero Bryan on page 75 and answer these questions.

1 Who does he design for?
2 What was the item of clothing that made him famous?
3 What is he studying at the moment?
4 According to Romero, what two things do you need to be a good designer?
5 What was the first item of clothing that he made?
6 Who were the first celebrities to wear his clothes?
7 For Romero, what's frustrating about being famous?

2 Without looking at the text again, say what these adjectives refer to.
Example: hottest – *pop stars*

1	outrageous	3	natural	5	overwhelming
2	eye-catching	4	trendy	6	unexpected

3 Work in a group. Think about clothes. Add as many words to each list as you can.

Pattern	**Material**	**Style**
stripy	silk	scruffy
plain		
floral		
patterned		
checked		
multicoloured		

4 Make lists of clothes you like and dislike. Use the words in Ex 3 to help you.

Likes	**Dislikes**
Plain coloured tops	*Multicoloured nylon shirts*

5 Work with a partner. Discuss which types of clothes you like and which you dislike. Use the words in Ex 3–4 to help you.

Example:
I'm not keen on multicoloured nylon shirts. I prefer woollen and cotton clothes with plain colours. I suit green. I can't stand baggy jeans. They look scruffy and untidy. How about you?

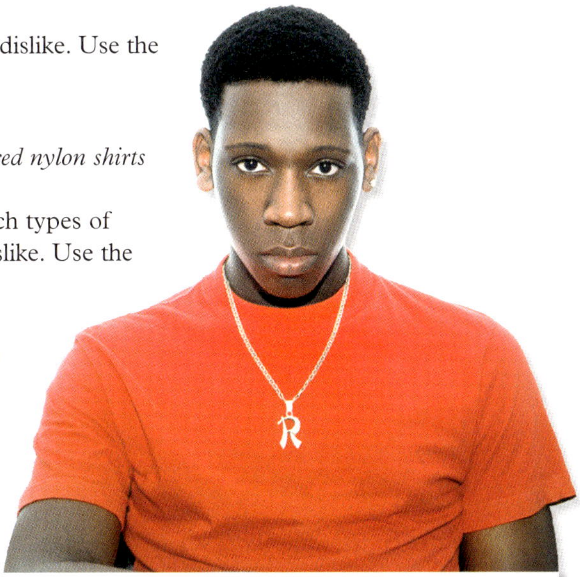

Hey, she's WEARING MY CLOTHES!

He was placed sixth in a list of under-21s most likely to become the richest people in Britain by 2020. Still in his teens, he has designed for some of the hottest stars in pop music. Who is he?

At home, joking with his sister **and** watching MTV dressed in black trousers and a T-shirt; Romero Bryan looks like a typical London teenager. He was doing his 'A' levels* when pop star Samantha Mumba made the front pages wearing one of his outrageous designs to the music industry's Brit Awards. It was this eye-catching dress, inspired by the way his 13-year-old sister Shamil wore a bath towel, that made his name. 'I only found out she'd worn it after my friends at school told me it was all over the front pages of the newspapers,' he says.

He was wearing the shirt at a club when he met pop duo Daphne and Celeste, who were impressed and put in an order. Bryan's cousin, Sabrina Washington, a member of *Mis-Teeq*, became another fan and, before long, he was juggling schoolwork with dressmaking at weekends.

'It was so overwhelming, so unexpected. I don't want to be a celebrity. I want to work for a fashion house when I graduate, but, even now, no-one wants to give me work experience because they already see me as a business. **But** I'm not – I'm just a boy. After all, I've still got lectures to go to.'

* 'A' levels are exams taken in the last year of school. They are pre-university exams.

Meanwhile, there's homework to be done. He is currently studying at the London School of Fashion. 'It feels as if I'm doing things backwards. As if I'm starting near the top and working my way down in order to bring myself up again.' So why bother? 'Everyone should have an education. It's great having natural talent, but **unless** you learn about the technical side, you can only go so far. Having a degree will show that I'm qualified to do what I'm doing.'

He wants to be treated like everyone else at college. **However**, it's unlikely that Bryan will be able to just blend in with the crowd with college staff handling his public relations, a trendy mobile phone voicemail message personally recorded by singer Kelis, and a diary full of photo shoots.

It's all a long way from his first attempt at shirt-making that began his career. 'The shirt came out twisted, with the arms too long and the seams inside-out. I didn't think I could wear it, but my mum said it was cool,' recalls Bryan. **So** he kept it.

Source: *Hey that's my dress she's wearing* by Deepah Shah for the *Observer*

LANGUAGE STUDY

Linking ideas

1 Look at these sentences from the text. Does *but* add a new point or contrast two points?

They already see me as a business. ***But*** *I'm not – I'm just a boy.*

2 Look at these lists of linking words in the text. Add the words in the box to the lists.

also	although	as a result	because	if	in addition	though	too

1 Contrast: *but, however* ______

2 Condition: *unless* ______

3 Cause and effect: *so* ______

4 Addition: *and* ______

3 Answer these questions about the words in the lists.

1 Which word is normally only used at the end of a sentence?
2 Which word can be used at the beginning, middle or end of a sentence?
3 Which words can't be used at the end of a sentence?

Grammar reference page 91

4 Join these pairs of sentences together to make single sentences. Use the words in brackets.

1 Two famous pop stars liked his shirt. They asked him to make clothes for them. (so)
2 He is studying at the London School of Fashion. He wants to learn about the technical side of designing. (because)
3 He gets his degree. He won't be able to prove that he's a qualified designer. (unless)

5 Rewrite these sentences using the words in brackets.

1 He was working hard to pass his 'A' level exams. He was making clothes in his free time. (also)
2 He is famous. He wants to be treated like the other students. (however)
3 He listened to his mum's advice. He wore his shirt and became famous. (as a result)

The order of adjectives

6 When there is more than one adjective before a noun, the adjectives should come in a certain order. What is the order of adjectives in the examples?

NOTE

It is unusual to have more than three adjectives before a noun.

Opinion →	Size →	Colour + pattern →	Origin →	Material →	Use →	Noun
1 *traditional*		*multicoloured*	*Scottish*			*kilt*
2 *elegant*	*long*					*dress*
3 *expensive*		*blue*		*denim*		*jacket*

Grammar reference page 91

7 Write the adjectives in the correct order.

1 a floral Chinese short dress
2 an silk Italian expensive scarf
3 a red and blue football nylon top
4 a plastic long blue and grey raincoat
5 a multicoloured trendy sports bag

8 Work with a partner. Sit back-to-back and describe what you can remember of your partner's clothes.

9 Work with a partner. Student A is going to a party and he / she wants to borrow some clothes from student B. A turn to page 93. B turn to page 96.

Confessions of a shopaholic

Listening and speaking

1 Complete these sentences with the words in the box.

designer	fashionable	flatter	outfit	shopaholic	versatile

1. I spend all my money on clothes. I love shopping. I'm a __________.
2. I prefer clothes which are made by people like Versace and Armani. I always choose __________ clothes.
3. I think it's important to wear up-to-date clothes and be __________.
4. When I go to parties I make sure that I wear my favourite __________.
5. I can't stand spending time choosing which clothes to wear. My favourite clothes are fine for either formal or informal occasions. I buy clothes that are __________.
6. I'm not vain, but I like clothes that make me look slimmer, or taller. It's important to choose clothes that __________ you.

2 Work with a partner. Which of the statements in Ex 1 are true for you? Which are true for your partner?

3 **08** Listen to Claire talking about fashion. Are these statements true or false?

1. She pays more attention to clothes than make-up. ☐
2. She mainly buys expensive designer clothes. ☐
3. She loves high heels. ☐
4. Her favourite outfit at the moment is a pair of trousers. ☐
5. She gets her ideas from fashion magazines. ☐
6. She loves the fashion for short skirts. ☐
7. She thinks fashion is really about being self-confident. ☐
8. She likes men to wear short-sleeved shirts and jeans. ☐

4 Listen again and complete the interviewer's questions.

1. How ______________________________ buy clothes?
2. If you had more money, would you rather buy lots of new clothes or____________ ______________________ ?
3. How would you ______________________________ you dress?
4. Do you have ______________________________?
5. How ______________________________ fashion trends?
6. Is there anything that ______________________________?
7. Whose ______________________________ do you most admire?
8. What clothes ______________________________?

5 Work with a partner. Ask and answer the questions in Ex 4. Do you have similar fashion habits and tastes?

6 Work with a partner. How vain are you? Student A turn to page 93. Student B turn to page 96. Complete the magazine survey.

CD-ROM For more activities go to **Time out Unit 3**

4 Globetrotting

LEARNING AIMS

- Can recognise verb + infinitive or *-ing* patterns
- Can use phrasal verbs for travel
- Can write a review

Lead-in

1 Work with a partner. Which of these trips would you most like to go on? Why?

- USA: with a city tour of New York
- Kenya: with a safari to a wildlife park
- Brazil: for the Rio de Janeiro carnival
- India: with a visit to the Taj Mahal
- Thailand: with a beach holiday

2 Which other countries would you really like to visit? Why?

Reading

1 **09** David Abram is one of the authors of the *Rough Guide to India*. Read the interview on page 79 and answer these questions.

1. How much time does he spend writing compared to travelling?
2. How does he feel at the end of his trips?
3. How does he feel when small villages become large holiday resorts?

2 Read the text again and choose the correct alternative.

1 One thing he loves about his job is:
- a that it forces him to have new experiences and opinions
- b the writing at the end of each journey
- c that he finds places normal tourists don't go to

2 He finds it difficult to make friends when he's travelling because:
- a he feels very lonely
- b he never stays in one place for long enough
- c he is too busy writing

3 Being a guidebook writer is very different to being on holiday because you:
- a go to places where you are likely to get ill
- b have to read other books by travel writers
- c spend the whole day working

4 He doesn't usually tell restaurants who he is because he:
- a doesn't want them to pay particular attention to him
- b doesn't want to spend time talking to the owners
- c already has all the details he needs about the local area

5 A good guidebook writer should love:
   a going on holiday
   b learning foreign languages
   c writing about other places

6 David:
   a pays for the travelling with his own money
   b gets paid some money before he goes travelling
   c gets paid his expenses when he comes back

Source: *Someone's got to do it: jobs in the Travel Industry* by Ben Wood for *The Independent*

Off the beaten track

WITH DAVID ABRAM

We asked Rough Guide author David Abram about his life writing travel guides for backpackers ...

What do you like and dislike about your job?
At the beginning it was tremendously exciting knowing that my opinions and experiences would **end up** in print. Also researching a book forced me to explore places that are **off the beaten track**, places I might not otherwise visit. However, it can get lonely. Sometimes I spend three or four months travelling on my own without the opportunity to hang around and forge relationships. Every time I get back I say to myself 'never again'. The next eight or nine months back at home writing can be a pretty intense experience too, with days spent in pyjamas, putting the work off.

Doesn't it feel like you're on holiday?
When you're abroad, it's the opposite of a holiday – you get up early and don't stop all day. Everything you see and feel may filter into the book, so it's important to remember to note down all the details. It's enjoyable but absolutely exhausting, and, when you're really tired, it's easy to get rundown or ill.

Do you try to remain undercover as much as possible?
Yes, but it's not always possible. I've done several books on Goa, so I'm pretty well known there. I try not to tell restaurants to avoid preferential treatment, but being known can sometimes be advantageous. **Chatting** with hoteliers can give me local details that make a guide seem less like it's written by someone just **passing through**. I also get a lot of people asking to be included, but you've got to write a dependable book, and that comes first.

Is there a danger that the places mentioned in guidebooks become spoiled?
It certainly happens, though it's difficult to say to what extent guidebooks are responsible for this. Writers like to exaggerate the impact of their work, but I think word of mouth is just as influential. Nevertheless, I've seen tiny fishing villages turn into big resorts, and that's a shame. I think guidebooks should try to encourage **sustainable** development not overdevelopment.

What qualities do you need to be a good Rough Guide writer?
It's essential that you enjoy going to new places and gathering information. You should be a bit like a sponge, absorbing all sorts of cultural and sociological information. And you must also love language – the nuts and bolts of writing. Mainly, though, you need to cope with being on your own and be able to put up with not having much money.

Is the pay that bad?
Yes! You get a portion of your **royalties** in advance, which just about covers your expenses on the trip, but not much more. After that it just depends how many people buy the book.

3 Explain the meaning of these words and phrases from the text.

1 end up	4 passing through
2 off the beaten track	5 sustainable
3 chatting	6 royalties

4 Work with a partner and discuss these questions.
   1 Would you like to write travel guides?
   2 What would you like and dislike about the job?
   3 Could you be married and do this job?

LANGUAGE STUDY

verb + infinitive or *-ing*

1 When one verb is followed by another verb, there are several possible patterns. Match these sentences to the patterns.

1	*Researching a book* ***forced me to explore*** *places.*	a	verb + *-ing* form
2	***Remember to note down*** *all the details.*	b	verb + object + *-ing* form
3	*I* ***spend three or four months travelling.***	c	verb + infinitive
4	*It's essential that you* ***enjoy going*** *to new places.*	d	verb + object + infinitive

Grammar reference page 91

2 Join the two parts of these sentences.

1 They arrived late and watched
2 If I go to Italy I'd like
3 I really enjoyed
4 Tomorrow evening my friend has promised
5 We were so happy in Spain that we didn't want
6 I arrived just in time to see

a you swimming with that girl.
b our holiday to end.
c to meet me at the hotel.
d to visit Rome and Venice.
e watching the village festival yesterday.
f their plane taking off without them.

3 Match the sentences in Ex 2 to the patterns in Ex 1.

4 Some verbs are normally followed by an infinitive:
He decided to go for a walk.
Others are normally followed by the *-ing* form:
She enjoyed travelling.
Complete the boxes with *infinitive* and *-ing*. Use the sentences in Ex 2 to help you.

Verb + ______________	**Verb +** ______________
hope, manage, offer, pretend, promise, refuse, want	finish, give up, practise, see, watch

5 Some verbs can be followed by the infinitive or the *-ing* form. With a few verbs, for example *stop*, *remember*, and *try*, this changes the meaning. Read the sentences. Whose friends received postcards? Whose friends didn't? Who was doing something else, and decided to send some postcards?

Danni: *I* ***stopped sending*** *postcards to my friends.*
Kerri: *I* ***stopped to send*** *some postcards to my friends.*

Grammar reference page 91

6 Complete these sentences to make them true for you. Compare your ideas with a partner.

1 Next year I'd like to give up ______________________________
2 In a month's time I hope ______________________________
3 I stopped ______________________________ last year.
4 I've never managed ______________________________
5 I don't enjoy ______________________________ anymore.
6 I've decided ______________________ before my next birthday.
7 I must practise ______________________________ more!
8 I don't want ______________________________ anymore.

Nightmare journeys

Phrasal verbs: travel

Vocabulary and listening

1 Work with a partner. Match the numbers in the picture above to phrasal verbs in the box.

drop off ______	flag down ______	get in ______	get off ______	get on ______
get out ______	pick up ______	queue up for ______	take off ______	

2 Work with a partner. Which of the phrasal verbs in Ex 1 can you use with these kinds of transport? Make lists.

1 bus: ______________________ 4 taxi: ______________________
2 car: ______________________ 5 train: ______________________
3 ferry: ______________________ 6 tram: ______________________

3 **10** Listen to the story about a nightmare journey. What do these numbers refer to in the story? **a** 3 **b** 130 **c** 5 **d** 4

4 Why was the journey a 'nightmare journey'?

5 Listen again. Tick all of the phrasal verbs in Ex 1 that you hear. Check your answers in Listening script 10 on page 95.

Speaking

1 What things can go wrong on a journey? Make a list. Compare your list with a partner.

2 You are going to describe a difficult journey you have made. It could be a long journey or a short one. Decide which journey you are going to describe.

3 Plan how you are going to describe your journey. Think about:

- When you made the journey
- Who you were with
- Where you were going
- What happened
- How you felt at the time
- How you feel about it now

4 Work with a partner. Describe your journey.

Writing

1 You are a travel writer. You are going to write a review about a place that you don't recommend anyone goes to for a holiday. Plan your review. Decide:

- Which place you are going to describe
- What things you want to write about. Examples: the food, the people, the town, the weather, the hotel, transport, prices
- The language you are going to use to make your review interesting to read. Examples: linking words such as *but*, *too*, *however*; using *quite*, *very* and *absolutely* with adjectives, and phrasal verbs to talk about travel

2 Write your review. Read other students' reviews and vote for the worst place.

CD-ROM For more activities go to **Time out Unit 4**

5 Review

Lead-in **1** Imagine you could be anywhere in the world. Where would you be? Work with a partner and answer these questions.

1 Where are you?
2 Are you alone or with someone else? Who?
3 What are you doing?
4 What's the weather like?
5 What are you wearing?
6 How do you feel?

Language study

1 Correct the mistakes in these emails.

To:
Cc:
Bcc:
Subject:

Hi John,

It seems ages since I saw you last. I've had a great summer so far.

As you know, we (1) *go* ___________ to Andalucia in southern Spain a few weeks ago. After the stress and long hours of accountancy exams it (2) *had been* ___________ wonderful to spend our days (3) *to do* ___________ yoga and sunbathing. We were very lucky with the weather. The week before we arrived it (4) *was being* ___________ cloudy. But during our time there it was very hot – 38 degrees! (5) *Unless* ___________ we didn't do much walking around. Instead, we just (6) *were relaxing* ___________ beside the (7) *swimming, blue, huge* ___________________ pool. You should try it sometime! It really was (8) *very* ___________ wonderful. The food was great, (9) *also* ___________.

See you soon,
Cathy

To:
Cc:
Bcc:
Subject:

Hi Elly,

We've been in Turkey for the last two weeks (10) *because* ___________ we are really enjoying (11) *to spend* ___________ time here. We've rented a (12) *old traditional white* ___________ villa that has an enormous balcony. The view over the sea's (13) *very* ___________ fantastic! Yesterday morning we (14) *had hired* ___________ a car and went out for the day. We (15) *had been driving* ___________ along the coast when we came across a beach with (16) *turquoise, beautiful* _______________ water. It looked really nice, (17) *in addition* ___________ in fact the water was (18) *absolutely* ___________ cool, so we didn't stay in long.

Best wishes,
Patrick

2 Complete these sentences with true statements about holidays you've taken. Compare your ideas with a partner.

1 On holiday last year I spent time _______________________________
2 I remember _______________________________________
3 My favourite place was a _______________________________
4 While _______________, I saw an interesting _______________________
5 Before I went to ___________ I'd never _______________________

Vocabulary

1 11 Read how to play 'Guess the word' and listen to the example.

2 Play the game.

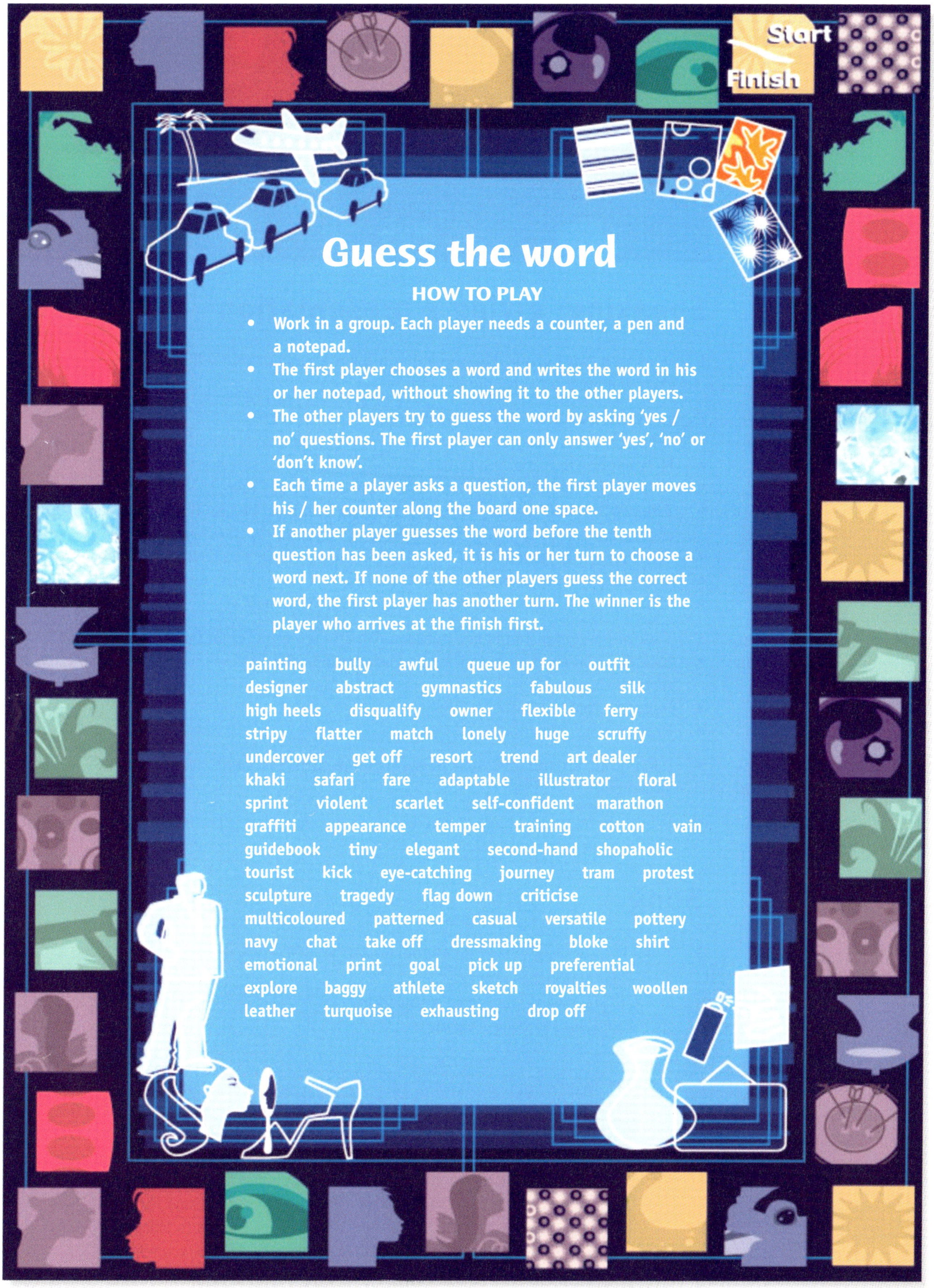

Speaking: giving a presentation

1 Work in a small group. You are going to plan a holiday and 'sell' it to the rest of the class. Follow the instructions.

Step 1: Choose your holiday

Discuss these questions and make decisions.

- What kind of holiday is it? (An activity holiday? A beach holiday? A cultural holiday?)
- How expensive is it going to be?
- What's the destination? (Where is it? How do you get there?)
- What accommodation is offered? (Hotel, guest house, bed and breakfast, self-catering, camping?)
- What food is included in the price? (How many meals a day? What kind of meals?)
- What facilities are available? (Is there a beach, a pool, sports facilities?)
- What other activities can you do? (Shopping? Walking?)

Step 2: Prepare your presentation

- Your presentation should last between five and ten minutes and each person must speak!
- Include an introduction and divide your presentation into sections (for example the sections in Step 1).
- Include a map or some pictures.
- Practise your presentation.

Step 3: Give your presentation

- Each group should give their presentation in turn. The other groups are the audience.

Step 4: Choose the best holiday

- When all the groups have finished, vote to decide which is the best holiday. You cannot choose your own holiday!

Song

1 Read the factfile about Dido and answer these questions.

1 What nationality is she?
2 Did she always plan to be a musician?
3 When did she become famous?

factfile

Dido Armstrong was born in North London on 25th December 1971 – Christmas Day! Her real name is Florian Cloud De Bounevialle Armstrong. She comes from an artistic family. Her mother is a poet and her brother Rollo is a musician, while her father is a publisher. She went to Birkbeck College in London to study law but got involved in the music business through Rollo. She became well-known all over the world when Eminem used part of her song *Thank you* in his huge number 1 hit *Stan*. She's now one of the music world's highest paid stars thanks to the success of her first two albums, *No Angel* and *Life for Rent*.

2 Work with a partner. Look at these words from the song and predict what you think the song is about. Share your ideas with the class.

unpack	forget	flat	sunset	sand	goodbye	work	mess	plane

3 **12** Listen to the song and check your predictions.

Sand in my shoes

Two weeks away feels like the whole world should've changed
But I'm home now and things still look the same
I think I'll leave it till tomorrow to unpack, try to forget for one more night
That I'm back in my flat
On the road where the cars never stop going through the night
To a life where I can't watch the sunset. I don't have time. I don't have time ...

Chorus

I've still got sand in my shoes and I can't shake the thought of you
I should get on, forget you but why would I want to?
I know we said goodbye – anything else would've been confused
But I want to see you again.

Tomorrow's back to work and down to sanity
Should run a bath and then clear up the mess I made before I left here
Try to remind myself that I was happy here before I knew that I could get
On the plane and fly away
From the road where the cars never stop going through the night
To a life where I can watch the sun set and take my time, take all our time.

Chorus

Two weeks away, all it takes, to change and turn me around. I've fallen
I walked away, and never said, that I wanted to see you again.

Chorus

4 Choose the correct alternative.

1 She doesn't unpack because she:
   a wants to forget reality
   b stayed up late to watch the sunset
   c doesn't have enough time to do it

2 She said goodbye to:
   a her friends at the airport
   b her boyfriend in another country
   c her old life

3 What is she going to do the next day?
   a get on another plane
   b go for a drive in her car
   c go to work

TIME OUT
Extra practice

Unit 1

1 Complete the crossword.

Clues

1 Alex Ferguson ____ David Beckham for Arsenal's second goal. (6)
2 This is what happens to you if you are caught taking drugs in competitions (12)
3 Say what you think is wrong or bad about something. (9)
4 This is when you use physical force to hurt people. (7)
5 After an argument, you need to do this. (4, 4)
6 Another name for a 100 metre race. (6)
7 You lose this when you get angry. (6)
8 Unforgettable. (9)
9 This word has two meanings:
   1 clothing that men wear.
   2 The result when both teams have the same points in a match.
10 You do this in a boat. (3)
11 Use bad words. (5)

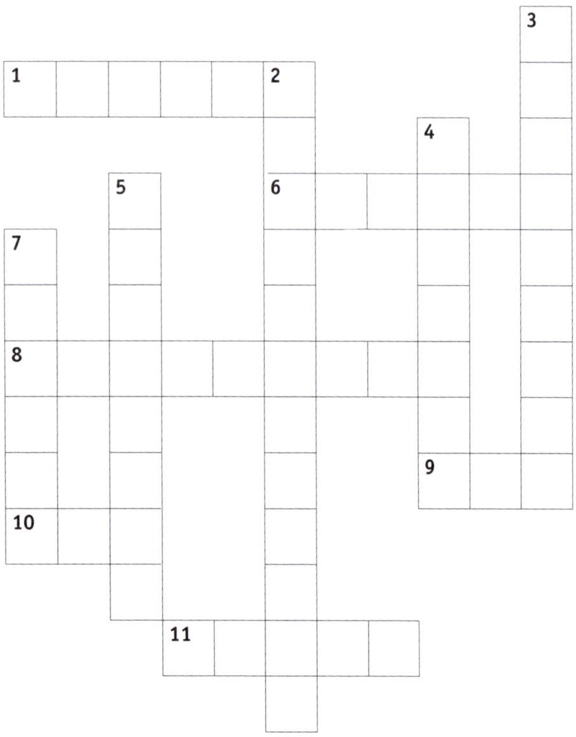

2 Choose the correct alternative.

1 *hit / score / raise* a goal
2 *play / run / take* the winning shot
3 *win / beat / score* a gold medal
4 *win / score / beat* the world record
5 *be disqualified from / withdraw / shut* a competition
6 *collect / make / take part in* an event

3 Complete the sentences with the past simple, past continuous or past perfect form of the verbs. Sometimes there is more than one possible answer.

1 After the trainer left, everybody (have) ________________ a rest.
2 By the time I got to the stadium, the match (already start) ________________.
3 When I saw him, he (stand) ________________ next to the ticket office.
4 I didn't need to buy any tickets as George (buy) ________________ them the day before.
5 Chelsea (beat) ________________ Manchester United 2–0 when we had to leave.
6 During the first half the team (play) ________________ really badly and everyone (criticise) ________________ the players. However, in the second half Robben (score) ________________ two goals and the crowd (become) ________________ much happier.

4 Complete the text about Zola Budd with the past simple, past continuous or past perfect form of the verbs.

Zola Budd was a top athlete. Before she came to the UK she (1 compete) ____________ in many events in South Africa and she (2 win) ____________ a lot of medals. She (3 become) ____________ a British Athlete because she (4 want) ____________ to take part in the 1984 Olympics. During the 3,000m final she (5 run) ____________ really well and many people thought she would win. However, as she (6 approach) ____________ one of the corners of the track she accidentally (7 hit) ____________ her main rival, Mary Decker-Slaney. Decker-Slaney (8 fall over) ____________ and she (9 be) ____________ disqualified. After the race she (10 lose) ____________ her temper and (11 accuse) ____________ Budd of cheating. Budd didn't win the race, though. The accident (12 upset) ____________ her and she only finished seventh.

Unit 2

1 Complete these sentences with *very* or *absolutely*.

1 The film was __________ good. In fact it was __________ fantastic.

2 My new camera is __________ tiny.

3 The artist's signature on this painting is __________ small.

4 Their new house is __________ wonderful, and the view across the countryside is __________ amazing.

5 This sculpture is __________ huge. It's over 20m high.

6 I'm afraid my experience at the art gallery was __________ bad. A thief stole my wallet.

2 For each sentence decide if *quite* means *a bit*, or *absolutely*.

1 The New York Museum of Modern Art is quite extraordinary. __________

2 The style of this painting is quite abstract. __________

3 The way the colours in this dress catch the light is quite amazing. __________

4 This pattern is quite interesting, but I prefer something more subtle. __________

3 Complete the dialogue with the phrases in the box.

absolutely fabulous	nothing for me	
prefer something more subtle	quite boring	
quite nice	really interesting	want to

Layla: Have you seen the latest exhibition of sculpture at the modern art museum?

Joe: Yes, I have, but it does (1) __________

Layla: Oh? Why's that? I think it's (2) __________ __________! I mean, I love the fact that it's all so completely abstract.

Joe: Well, I suppose it's (3) __________, but I (4) __________. For example, I watched an artist painting along the river, the other day. The use of contrasting shades in her work made it (5) __________.

Layla: I'm afraid I think pictures of the countryside are (6) __________. They make me (7) __________ fall asleep. I prefer modern art.

4 Complete the names of the different shades and colours.

1

dull ______ blue
n ______ blue
d ______ blue
b ______ blue
l ______ blue

2

p ______
t ______
k ______
b ______
s ______

5 Read Emma's description of the Eiffel tower and underline the adjectives that are used to describe it.

The Eiffel Tower is probably the most famous and distinctive building in Paris, but before I saw it for the first time, when I was about 23, I had thought of it as an unimpressive piece of grey metal. Obviously it had been a contemporary design back in the nineteenth century when it was built, but even then, most Parisians had hated it. And it did nothing for me. So when I first went to Paris I didn't rush to visit it. Then one day the friend I was with insisted that we went to see it. We got out of the Metro and turned a corner and there it was. It was huge! What surprised me was that it had a colour, a kind of dull brown. The base of it was reassuringly large and made the whole structure look secure. Then there was the beauty of the iron work. It was so delicate. Look up and up and up and finally you see the top. It has no function, but perhaps that's part of the attraction. I love it!

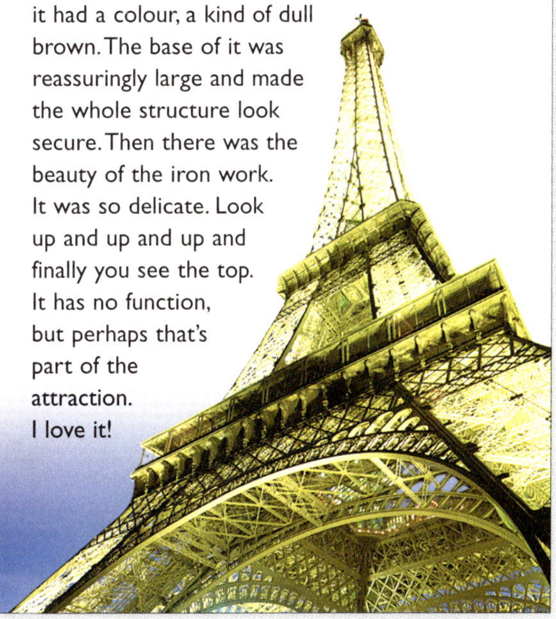

6 Make lists with the adjectives you underlined in Exercise 5.

General appearance and reputation: *famous* __________

Size and colour: __________

7 Think about a building you particularly like. Make lists of adjectives similar to the lists in Ex 6.

Unit 3

1 Look at the lists. Find the words which are in the incorrect list and rewrite them in the correct list.

Opinion / style	**Colour / pattern**	**Material**
baggy	checked	cotton
black	nylon	plain
silk	casual	stripy
smart	patterned	scruffy
tight	woollen	leather
________	________	________
________	________	________
	________	________

2 Describe the clothes in the pictures using the words in Ex 1 to help you.

Example: *a scruffy checked cotton shirt*

3 Describe the clothes you are wearing now and those of a friend you saw today.

1 I'm wearing ______________________________

____

2 My friend was wearing ______________________________

____

4 Complete the text about models with the linking words in the box.

and · as a result · because · however · so · though · unless

Most models have only a short career (1) ________ they have to look young all the time. (2) ________, some models such as Claudia Schiffer and Naomi Campbell have been able to work for many years. This is fairly unusual, (3) ________.

In the 1980s, the designer Versace, and eventually other designers, began to pay some models like Campbell and Schiffer large sums of money to model his clothes, (4) ________ these models became known as 'supermodels'. It's said that one of them, Linda Evangelista, refused to get out of bed in the morning (5) ________ she was paid at least $10,000! (6) ________, towards the end of the 1990s many designers began to think that supermodels were too expensive. (7) ________ they employed cheaper ones, and found that their fashion shows were still successful. Is the era of the supermodel over?

Unit 4

1 Complete Rachel's email with the infinitive or *-ing* form of the verbs in the box.

be carry come back fit give have
pretend see stay take try write

To:
Cc:
Bcc:
Subject: Re: Party

Hi Emily,

Thanks for your message. I'm really sorry I didn't make it to the party last night. The truth is I've been so busy getting ready for our big trip that I was just too tired to do anything. So I decided (1) ______________ an early night. Hope you had fun!

Just a few hours to go now! I'm really excited and can't wait (2) ______________ in South Africa again. There have been a few last minute problems like realising I hadn't finished (3) ______________ that essay I was meant to hand in next week – luckily I phoned my tutor and got an extension! Then, this morning we heard that Helen – my friend who we were planning (4) ______________ with in Cape Town is going away for a few days! I thought it was a joke at first! Fortunately, Helen's sister has promised (5) ______________ us the key to her flat. I've also been doing some last minute shopping. As we're travelling around a bit, and I hate (6) ______________ a heavy bag, I've bought some special lightweight travel clothes. They're not very elegant but I don't care if I look scruffy as long as I'm comfortable. I also bought myself one of those tiny digital cameras because I want (7) ______________ with lots of photos. Now I've just got to work out how to use it!

Andrew, on the other hand, likes (8) ______________ as much as possible on holiday! I think he enjoys (9) ______________ he's Indiana Jones or something. He's got a huge rucksack full of useless stuff like a tent (no way am I sleeping in a tent), a mosquito net, a penknife, and a portable radio. He'll never manage (10) ______________ everything in. Oh well, he'll soon give up (11) ______________ and realise I was right and he was wrong.

Anyway, hope (12) ______________ you soon after we get back.

Love
Rachel

2 Complete the phrasal verbs.

1 The taxi dropped me ______ at the terminal, 30 minutes before my flight.
2 At the security check I had to queue ______ five minutes.
3 I fell asleep, completely exhausted, as the plane took ______.
4 My cousin picked me ______ to take me to the airport 45 minutes late!
5 I got ______ the plane as the engines were starting. I was the last passenger.
6 We got ______ the car and flagged ______ a passing taxi.
7 As soon as I'd shown my passport I set _____ for the flight gate and arrived just in time.
8 His car broke ______ 2 km from the airport.

3 Change the order of the sentences in Ex 2 to make a story about catching a flight.

Start: _4_, ___, ___, ___, ___, ___, ___, ___ Finish

4 Find words from this unit in the wordsearch.

5 x kinds of transport
10 x phrasal verbs
1 word and 1 phrase from the reading text on page 79.
→ x 5, ↑ x 2, ↓ x 2, ↗ x 5, ↘ x 3

C	F	L	A	G	D	O	W	N	V	E
B	O	D	R	O	P	O	F	F	L	H
P	E	P	C	H	E	L	N	B	I	A
S	E	A	E	A	E	O	A	X	X	N
N	O	R	T	W	T	N	A	T	I	P
I	G	H	C	E	I	T	Z	A	P	I
T	E	E	G	A	N	T	R	U	M	C
E	T	C	T	X	A	T	H	A	P	K
G	O	S	G	O	S	E	R	D	R	U
P	U	T	O	F	F	T	G	A	A	P
S	T	A	B	U	S	F	A	N	C	D
Q	U	E	U	E	U	P	F	O	R	K

Grammar reference

Unit 1

Describing past events

You can talk about the past using different tenses:

Past simple

Form

Regular verbs

Add *-ed*	*explain* → *explained*
Ending in *-e*, add *-d*	*arrive* → *arrived*
Ending in consonant + *-y*, change *-y* to *-ied*	*study* → *studied*
Ending in a stressed vowel + consonant, double the consonant and add *-ed*	*grab* → *grabbed*

Irregular verbs

You need to learn the past simple forms of irregular verbs. Examples:

go → *went*	*see* → *saw*	*take* → *took*
have → *had*	*shut* → *shut*	*win* → *won*
hit → *hit*		

Statement:
Last week they ***arrived*** *in Athens.*

Negative statement:
They ***didn't arrive*** *in Athens because of bad weather.*

Question:
When ***did*** *they* ***arrive*** *in Athens?*

Use

The past simple is sometimes described as the 'normal' tense to talk about the past when there's no particular reason for using one of the other tenses. You use it to describe completed actions in a period of time in the past. This period of time is either directly referred to or is obvious:

I ***finished*** *that book last night. Then I* ***went*** *to bed.*
Did *you* ***take*** *any photos? (while you were on holiday)*

Past continuous

Form

I He She It	was	listening
You We They	were	listening

Statement:
He ***was watching*** *TV when the bell rang.*

Negative statement:
He ***wasn't doing*** *anything when I saw him.*

Question:
What ***was*** *he* ***doing*** *when you saw him?*

Use

You use the past continuous to describe an action that was happening at the time another event took place:
I ***was watching*** *a football match when I began to feel faint.*

You often use it to give background information in a narrative:
The sun ***was shining*** *and the birds* ***were singing*** *as the couple walked next to the river.*

Past perfect

Form

I, You, He, She, It, We, They	had	left

Statement:
When I arrived at the party Sheila ***had*** *already* ***gone****.*

Negative statement:
They ***hadn't been*** *to London before I took them last year.*

Question:
Had *you* ***met*** *her before I introduced her to you?*

Use

You use the past perfect when you want to make it clear that one action in the past happened before another action in the past.
In the sentence:

By the time I got to the party Jenny ***had left****.*
there are two actions in the past.

1 Jenny left
2 I arrived at the party

You use the past perfect to make it clear that 1 happened before 2.

Unit 2

Qualifying adjectives

very and *absolutely*

You can qualify adjectives by using words like *very* and *absolutely*. Most adjectives can follow *very*. These are called *gradable adjectives*. Some adjectives can't follow *very*. You can use *absolutely* with these ungradable adjectives.

very **+ gradable adjectives**	***absolutely*** **+ ungradable adjectives**
bad	enormous
big	extraordinary
good	fantastic
important	huge
interesting	perfect
nice	terrible
poor	tiny
rich	vital
small	wonderful

quite

Quite has got two very different meanings. When you use it before gradable adjectives its meaning is similar to *a bit*. When you use it before ungradable adjectives its meaning is similar to *absolutely*.

Unit 3

Linking ideas

You can use linking words to join different ideas together. Using linking words makes the presentation of your ideas more interesting and easier to understand. They have a number of different functions:

Function	Linking words
Addition	also, and, in addition, too
Cause and effect	as a result, because, so
Condition	if, unless
Contrast	although, but, however, though

You can use many of these linkers either at the start or the middle of sentences:

Although *I know it's no longer fashionable, I still wear that skirt I bought last year.*

I still wear that skirt I bought last year, ***although*** *I know it's no longer fashionable.*

Too can only be used at the end of a sentence. *Also, and, because, so, if, unless, although,* and *but* cannot be used at the end of a sentence. *Though* can be used in the beginning, middle or the end of a sentence.

Unit 4

Verb + infinitive or *-ing*

When one verb is followed by another verb, there are several possible patterns:

1 verb + *-ing* form:
I enjoy reading travel books.

2 verb + object + *-ing* form:
They watched him fishing from his boat.

3 verb + infinitive:
Writers like to exaggerate how important their work is.

4 verb + object + infinitive:
He reminded him to drink lots of water.

Some verbs are normally followed by the infinitive. Others are normally followed by the *-ing* form.

verb + infinitive	**verb + *-ing* form**
agree	can't stand
choose	don't mind
decide	enjoy
forget	finish
hope	give up
learn	hate
manage	practise
need	see
offer	watch
pretend	
promise	
refuse	
want	

Some verbs can be followed by the infinitive or the *-ing* form. Usually the meaning is the same, but with a few verbs, the meaning changes.

verb + infinitive or *-ing* (little or no change of meaning)	**verb + *-ing* or infinitive (change of meaning)**
continue	remember
like	stop
love	try
prefer	
start	

Wordlist

*** the 2,500 most common English words, ** very common words, * fairly common words

Unit 1
accuse *v* /ə'kju:z/ ***
allow *v* /ə'laʊ/ ***
apologise *v* /ə'pɒlə,dʒaɪz/ **
back down *v* /,bæk 'daʊn/
basketball *n* /'bɑ:skɪt,bɔ:l/ *
beat up *v* /bi:t ʌp/
bloke *n* /bləʊk/ **
bully *n* /'bʊli/ *
calm down *v* /,kɑ:m 'daʊn/
change your mind *phrase* /tʃeɪndʒ jə maɪnd/
collapse *v* /kə'læps/ **
compete *v* /kəm'pi:t/ ***
criticise *v* /'krɪtɪ,saɪz/ **
cruel *adj* /'kru:əl/ **
disgrace *n* /dɪs'greɪs/
disqualify *v* /dɪs'kwɒlɪ,faɪ/
dressing room *n* /'dresɪŋ ,ru:m/
enthusiastic *adj* /ɪn,θju:zi'æstɪk/ **
fault *n* /fɔ:lt/ ***
go for *v* /'gəʊ fɔ:/
gymnastics *n* /dʒɪm'næstɪks/
hold someone back *v* /,həʊld sʌmwʌn 'bæk/
incident *n* /'ɪnsɪdənt/ ***
javelin *n* /'dʒæv(ə)lɪn/
let down *v* /,let 'daʊn/
long jump *n* /'lɒŋ ,dʒʌmp/
lose control *v* /,lu:z kən'trəʊl/
marathon *n* /'mærəθən/ *
match *n* /mætʃ/ ***
memorable *adj* /'mem(ə)rəbl/
own up *v* /,əʊn 'ʌp/
participate *v* /pɑ:'tɪsɪ,peɪt/ **
pressure *n* /'preʃə/ ***
professional *adj* /prə'feʃnəl/ ***
protest *v* /prə'test/ **
rage *n* /reɪdʒ/ *
relay *n* /'ri:leɪ/
represent *v* /,reprɪ'zent/ ***
rivalry *n* /'raɪvlri/
rowing *n* /'rəʊɪŋ/
sailing *n* /'seɪlɪŋ/
score *v* /skɔ:/ ***
skiing *n* /'ski:ɪŋ/
sprint *n* /sprɪnt/ *
supporter *n* /sə'pɔ:tə/ ***
swear *v* /sweə/ **
take drugs *v* /,teɪk 'drʌgz/
take the blame *v* /,teɪk ðə 'bleɪm/
temper *n* /'tempə/ **
tragedy *n* /'trædʒədi/ **
training *n* /'treɪnɪŋ/ ***
treatment *n* /'tri:tmənt/ ***
violent *adj* /'vaɪələnt/ **
withdraw *v* /wɪð'drɔ:/ ***

Unit 2
absolutely *adj* /,æbsə'lu:tli/ ***
abstract *adj* /'æbstrækt/ **
achieve *v* /ə'tʃi:v/ ***
adaptable *adj* /ə'dæptəbl/
art dealer *n* /'ɑ:t ,di:lə/
artwork *n* /'ɑ:twɜ:k/
awful *adj* /'ɔ:fl/ **
beige *adj* /beɪʒ/
commercial *adj* /kə'mɜ:ʃl/
contemporary *adj* /kən'temp(ə)rəri/ ***
contrast *n* /'kɒntrɑ:st/ ***
curves *n* /kɜ:vz/ **
dark *adj* /dɑ:k/ ***
devalue *v* /di:'vælju:/
distinctive *adj* /dɪ'stɪŋktɪv/ **
dull *adj* /dʌl/ **
emotional *adj* /ɪ'məʊʃn(ə)l/ ***
extraordinary *adj* /ɪk'strɔ:dn(ə)rɪ/ **
expression *n* /ɪk'spreʃn/ ***
fabulous *adj* /'fæbjʊləs/ *
fascinating *adj* /'fæsɪneɪtɪŋ/ **
flexible *adj* /'fleksəbl/ **
graffiti *n* /grə'fi:ti/
greedy *adj* /'gri:di/ *
huge *adj* /hju:dʒ/ ***
illustrator *n* /'ɪlə,streɪtə/
impressed *adj* /ɪm'prest/
influence *v* /'ɪnfluəns/ ***
khaki *adj* /'kɑ:ki/
navy *adj* /'neɪvi/
network *v* /'netwɜ:k/ *
painting *n* /'peɪntɪŋ/ ***
pottery *n* /'pɒtəri/ *
print *n* /prɪnt/ **
produce *v* /prə'dju:s/ ***
purple *adj* /'pɜ:pl/ *
sales presentation *n* /'seɪlz ,prezn,teɪʃn/
scarlet *adj* /'skɑ:lət/ *
sculpture *n* /'skʌlptʃə/ **
shade *n* /ʃeɪd/ **
shape *n* /ʃeɪp/ ***
sketch *n* /sketʃ/ *
statue *n* /'stætʃu:/ *
style *n* /staɪl/ ***
subtle *adj* /'sʌtl/ **
suspicious *adj* /sə'spɪʃəs/ **
terrible *adj* /'terəbl/ ***
tiny *adj* /'taɪni/ ***
turquoise *adj* /'tɜ:kwɔɪz/
unexpected *adj* /,ʌnɪk'spektɪd/ **
vibrant *adj* /'vaɪbrənt/
wealthy *adj* /'welθi/ **

Unit 3
anti-aging treatments *n*
/,ænti'eɪdʒɪŋ ,tri:tmənts/
appearance *n* /ə'pɪərəns/ ***
attempt *v* /ə'tempt/ ***
baggy *adj* /'bægi/
blend in *v* /,blend 'ɪn/
casual *adj* /'kæʒuəl/ **
character *n* /'kærɪktə/ ***
checked *adj* /tʃekt/
compliment *n* /'kɒmplɪmənt/ *
cotton *adj* /'kɒtn/ **
designer *n* /dɪ'zaɪnə/ **
dressmaking *n* /'dres,meɪkɪŋ/
elegant *adj* /'elɪgənt/ **
eye-catching *adj* /'aɪ,kætʃɪŋ/
fashionable *adj* /'fæʃnəbl/ **
flatter *adj* /'flætə/
floral *adj* /'flɔ:rəl/
frustrating *adj* /frʌ'streɪtɪŋ/ *
get rid of *v* /get rɪd əv/
graduate *v* /'grædʒu,eɪt/ *
high heels *n* /,haɪ 'hi:lz/
individual *adj* /,ɪndɪ'vɪdʒuəl/ ***
inside-out *adj* /,ɪnsaɪd'aʊt/ *
kilt *n* /kɪlt/
make-up *n* /'meɪkʌp/ *
multicoloured *adj* /,mʌltɪ'kʌləd/
natural *adj* /'nætʃ(ə)rəl/ ***
nylon *adj* /'naɪlɒn/ *
occasion *n* /ə'keɪʒn/
outfit *n* /'aʊtfɪt/ *
outrageous *adj* /aʊt'reɪdʒəs/ *
overwhelming *adj* /,əʊvə'welmɪŋ/ *
patterned *adj* /'pæt(ə)nd/
plain *adj* /pleɪn/ *
plastic *adj* /'plæstɪk/ ***
plastic surgery *n* /,plæstɪk 'sɜ:dʒəri/
public relations *n* /,pʌblɪk rɪ'leɪʃnz/ *
qualified *adj* /'kwɒlɪ,faɪd/ **
scruffy *adj* /'skrʌfi/
second-hand *adj* /,sekənd'hænd/ *
self-confident *adj* /,self'kɒnfɪd(ə)nt/
shopaholic *n* /,ʃɒpə'hɒlɪk/
short-sleeved *adj* /,ʃɔ:t'sli:vd/
silk *n* /sɪlk/ **
smart *adj* /smɑ:t/ **
stripy *adj* /'straɪpi/
suit *v* /su:t/ ***
sunbed *n* /'sʌn,bed/
traditional *adj* /trə'dɪʃn(ə)l/ ***
treat someone like ... *v* /'tri:t sʌmwʌn ,laɪk/
trend *n* / trendy *adj* /trend/ /trendi/ ***
untidy *adj* /ʌn'taɪdi/
up-to-date *adj* /,ʌptə'deɪt/ *
vain *adj* /veɪn/ *
versatile *adj* /'vɜ:sə,taɪl/ *
wool *n* /woollen *adj* /wʊl **/ /'wʊlən/ *

Unit 4
absorb *v* /əb'zɔ:b/ **
advantageous *adj* /,ædvən'teɪdʒəs/
chat *v* /tʃæt/ **
cope with *v* /'kəʊp ,wɪð/ ***
crash into *v* /'kræʃ ,ɪntu:/
dependable *adj* /dɪ'pendəbl/
drop off *v* /,drɒp 'ɒf/
encourage *v* /ɪn'kʌrɪdʒ/ ***
end up *v* /,end 'ʌp/
exaggerate *v* /ɪg'zædʒə,reɪt/ *
exhausting *adj* /ɪg'zɔ:stɪŋ/
expense *n* /ɪk'spens/ ***
experience *n* /ɪk'spɪəriəns/ ***
explore v /ɪk'splɔ:/ ***
fare *n* /feə/ **
festival *n* /'festɪvl/ ***
flag down *v* /,flæg 'daʊn/
force *v* /fɔ:s/ ***
get in *v* /,get 'ɪn/
get off *v* /,get 'ɒf/
get on *v* /,get 'ɒn/
get out *v* /,get 'aʊt/
give up *v* /,gɪv 'ʌp/
guidebook *n* /'gaɪd,bʊk/ *
haggle *v* /'hægl/
hang around *v* /,hæŋ ə'raʊnd/
holiday resort *n* /'hɒlɪdeɪ rɪ,zɔ:t/
intense *adj* /ɪn'tens/ **
journey *n* /'dʒɜ:ni/ ***
lonely *adj* /'ləʊnli/
nightmare *n* /'naɪt,meə/ **
note down *v* /nəʊt daʊn/
off the beaten track *phrase*
/,ɒf ðə ,bi:tn 'træk/
owner *n* /'əʊnə/ ***
pass through *v* /,pɑ:s 'θru:/
pay attention to *v* /,peɪ ə'tenʃn tu:/
pick up *v* /,pɪk 'ʌp/
preferential treatment *n*
/,prefə,renʃl 'tri:tmənt/
pretend *v* /prɪ'tend/ **
put off *v* /,pʊt 'ɒf/
queue up for *v* /,kju: 'ʌp fə/
refuse *v* /rɪ'fju:z/ ***
royalties *n* /'rɔɪəltɪz/ *
rundown *adj* /,rʌn'daʊn/
safari *n* /sə'fɑ:ri/
shocked *adj* /ʃɒkt/ *
spoiled *adj* /spɔɪld/
squeeze in *v* /,skwi:z 'ɪn/
sustainable *adj* /sə'steɪnəbl/
take off *v* /,teɪk 'ɒf/
tram *n* /træm/
tremendously *adv* /trə'mendəsli/
trip *n* /trɪp/ ***
undercover *adj* /,ʌndə'kʌvə/
word of mouth *phrase* /wɜ:d əv maʊθ/

Communication activities

Student A

Unit 3, Language study Ex 9 page 77

If you are a man, look at picture 1. If you are a woman, look at picture 2.
Choose what you want to borrow (you must choose at least 4 items and describe them to B).

1

2

Unit 3, Listening and speaking Ex 6 page 77

1 Read this part of the questionnaire and answer the questions.
2 Ask student B the questions and make a note of his / her answers.
3 Answer student B's questions.

How vain are you?

1 How much time do you spend on your appearance in the morning?
  - **a** 10–20 minutes
  - **b** 21–45 minutes
  - **c** Over 45 minutes

2 How often do you buy new clothes?
  - **a** Once every 6 months
  - **b** Once a month
  - **c** Once a week

3 If someone gives you a compliment, how do you react?
  - **a** I wonder what they want from me
  - **b** I feel flattered but I don't believe that they mean it
  - **c** I usually believe that they mean what they say

4 Do you have photographs of yourself in your bedroom?
  - **a** No
  - **b** Yes, but only me with my friends and family
  - **c** Yes, including ones of just me that I like

5 Have you ever been on a sunbed?
  - **a** No, never
  - **b** Yes, a few times
  - **c** Yes, many times

4 Compare your answers. If your answers are mainly 'a' you aren't at all vain. If your answers are mainly 'b' you are quite vain, but this is normal. If your answers are mainly 'c' you are too vain!

Listening scripts

Unit 1 Crossing the line

Listening script 01

Reading text from page 67

Listening script 02

(S = Sarah; J = Jenny; B = Ben)

S: Oh look they're doing one of those ten most memorable sporting moments on the TV – this time with the Olympic Games.

J: The ten most memorable moments, crikey that's difficult, there are so many!

S: Yeah, you're supposed to phone in with your top three and then they select the top ten entries.

J: Shall we do it?

B: Yeah, I'm up for it. Who shall we start with?

J: Well, there's Steve Redgrave's fifth gold medal for rowing in five games; that was a pretty fantastic moment especially when you think he had been suffering from diabetes at the time of his last one in Sydney.

B: Yes I remember staying up at night to watch that. Did you know he had to inject himself six times a day, every day … and still does I suppose.

S: Nadia Comaneci was one of my favourites; she was only 14 when she won three gold medals for gymnastics.

J: I don't think 14 year olds should be allowed to take part in the Olympics. Think of the pressure. What sort of life is it for a child? I mean think of the training she must've had to do!

B: Anyway it wasn't really a great moment, was it? I remember reading about this Italian marathon runner way back in 1908. Dorando Pietri was his name. Apparently he was inside the stadium some way in front of everyone else when he collapsed four times and got up each time. The last time he was helped across the line by two officials. He was disqualified, poor bloke, even though he hadn't asked for help.

J: Yes, I read that story recently. Apparently one of the officials who helped him was probably Arthur Conan Doyle, you know, the guy who wrote Sherlock Holmes.

B: Really? I didn't know that. But you're forgetting the best of all.

S: What's that?

B: The 100 metres in Seoul; it's such a dramatic story. It was really about the rivalry between two very different people. There was Carl Lewis, a great Olympian, rather arrogant, someone who never stopped talking, and Ben Johnson a dark, brooding figure who found it extremely difficult to face the media. They came head to head in the final and most people thought Lewis would win again. However, after an amazing start, Johnson won in 9.79 seconds, a world record which has never been beaten – and Canada went crazy with joy. And then there was news later that night that he'd been taking drugs. I'll never forget that ... it was greatness and tragedy all in one event.

J: And Lewis got the gold didn't he?

B: Yep, Lewis got the gold and Johnson fled back to Canada in disgrace.

S: The Olympics can be quite political. Do you remember those two black Americans, Tommie Smith and John Carlos, who, when they were collecting their medals, raised a black glove in the air to protest about the treatment of black people? They were sent home the next day by the American Olympic committee ...

Unit 2 Is it art?

Listening script 03 and 04

(I = Interviewer; B = Basher)

I: Simon, could I ask you about how you started as an artist? You trained as a graphic designer. When you left university, did you work immediately as a graphic designer?

B: I started work as an illustrator first of all. I did about a year or so but then I went into the music industry.

I: And what did you do? Were you a musician?

B: Yes. At first I was in a band. We had a small record deal and we toured. Then I became a session musician, and later on I went into management, basically looking after a collection of pop bands and record producers.

I: Has that influenced your work as an artist or in the way you sell your art?

B: When I worked in the music industry I wasn't sure how to network with other people or how to conduct myself. Through the mistakes I made, I learnt how to push myself forward and be more adaptable when meeting new people.

I: So how did you become an independent artist?

B: Well, I was still working as a manager, not really enjoying it very much, when a friend told me about a place called Spitalfields market, where artists selling contemporary stuff can rent a cheap stall. I drew the first thing that came into my head, some Japanese characters, photocopied and enlarged them, stuck them on some wood and put them on the wall at the market. And that was it. In the first week I had some really excellent sales and so I decided to carry on.

• • •

I: OK. Now the images you produce are very distinctive. Tell us about them.

B: Stylistically they're graphic images, with influences from graffiti and comics. I'm really interested in drawing people's characters, particularly their expressions. I try to make my images as simple as possible but with lots of emotional content.

I: I suppose your prints could be used for virtually anything?

B: Yes, all the images are basically created on a computer, so that they can be transferred to any medium; for example, clothing such as t-shirts. Or you can use them for computer games – for anything really.

I: Why do you think you're successful?

B: I think it's being flexible. A lot of artists are a bit set in their ways, not very open to other people's ideas or usages for their work because they're worried about being too commercial. I don't mind selling my work in different mediums, not just paintings, and I don't feel this is devaluing it. It's important to get the balance right. I'm an artist, but I'm also a businessman.

I: What advice would you give somebody who wants to become an artist?

B: I think you have to be honest with yourself and do what you enjoy, because it's difficult to make a living from art. If you hit on something which is working then follow it up and stay focused on that.

I: Finally, your real name is Simon. Where does the name Basher come from?

B: Basher is an old fashioned name for a school bully, and I thought these characters were so unlike that. So it was a bit of a joke really and it just stuck.

Listening script 05

Pronunciation Ex 1 page 73

Listening script 06

Reading text from page 73

Unit 3 Fashion victims

Listening script 07

Reading text from page 75

Listening script 08

(I = Interviewer; C = Claire)

I: So Claire, how often do you buy clothes?

C: Well as often as possible, actually. I'm a bit of a shopaholic. I don't spend nearly as much time or money on my hair. And I rarely wear make-up. But, to me, clothes are a really important part of my appearance. For that reason I do buy a lot of clothes, yeah.

I: If you had more money would you rather buy lots of new clothes or a few expensive ones?

C: Well, I'm not sure really, erm the cost of clothes is not really important to me. I like something, I buy it. I mean I've bought second-hand clothes, I've bought designer clothes. So I'm not sure about that.

I: How would you describe the way you dress – your style?

C: I wouldn't say I follow fashion. Erm, I think I'm quite individual. I like to find clothes that no one else will have. However, I also like to be comfortable. I rarely wear high heels and I hate being hot, so this affects what I wear.

I: Do you have a favourite outfit?

C: Well I mean it changes from time to time. At the moment I've got a favourite pair of trousers that I seem to be wearing all the time, to everywhere, with everything. Erm, they're very versatile so I can wear them with trainers or high heels, erm different belts and tops. They can be smart or casual.

I: How aware are you of current fashion trends?

C: Not particularly. I mean, I don't watch fashion shows on TV and I don't read fashion magazines. So really my only exposure to fashion is when ... when I'm shopping or in the street when I see someone else wearing something. I think that fashion is quite hard to avoid. You're often not aware that you are aware.

I: Is there anything that you wouldn't wear?

C: Erm, I try not to wear anything that doesn't flatter me. I very rarely wear short skirts because I hate my legs. I also never wear anything too revealing as that's just not my style.

I: Whose sense of fashion or style do you most admire?
C: I really admire Cameron Díaz. I think everybody does. She's always very confident in the way she dresses and I think that's the most important thing. That's what fashion's about – having your own self-confidence.
I: And what about for a man? What clothes do you like for a man?
C: Well, I think it comes down to what I don't like men wearing. So it's things like white socks, sandals and trousers that are too short. I don't like short-sleeved shirts with jeans as all the guys wear them and they just all look the same. I like a man to look good, but not as if he has tried really hard. That's not too much to ask for, is it?

Unit 4 Globetrotting

Listening script 09

Reading text from page 79

Listening script 10

My boyfriend and I had decided to spend a nice romantic three-day weekend in Prague. We managed to get to the airport on time. The plane **took off** and landed on time, and our baggage didn't get lost. The nightmare began when we **flagged down** a taxi from the airport. After haggling to agree a reasonable fare, we set off towards the city centre. The first thing we noticed was that there were no seatbelts, which was very unfortunate as the guy was doing 130 kilometres an hour while singing along to Kylie Minogue. It was no surprise that five minutes later he crashed into the back of a lorry at some traffic lights. Luckily we were OK. Unluckily he said that we had to **get out** and that he couldn't take us any further. But he said that he'd radioed his friend, who was also on his way into the city, and that he would **pick** us **up**. We noticed that his friend had a full taxi already. This, however, didn't seem to be a problem and we were asked to squeeze in anyway. We ended up sat on top of a couple of elderly German tourists and their four-year-old grandson. They were just as shocked as us. We finally made it into the city centre, and, not surprisingly, got **dropped off** at the wrong hotel.

Unit 5 Review

Listening script 11

(A–D = game players)
A: OK, my turn. I've thought of a word.
B: Is the word a noun?
A: No. One.
C: Erm … Is it an adjective?
A: Yes. Two.
D: Is it a material for clothes?
A: No. Three.
B: Is it a colour?
A: Yes. Four.
C: Is it khaki?
A: No. Five.
D: Is it turquoise?
A: Yes. Six. Your turn.
[pause]
D: OK. I've chosen one …

Listening script 12

Song from page 85

Communication activities

Student B

Unit 3, Language study Ex 9 page 77

If you are a man, look at picture 1. If you are a woman, look at picture 2.
A is going to ask you for some items from your wardrobe. Look carefully at the clothes you are asked for. Is it possible for you to lend them? Look at the notes and if not, give a reason and suggest alternatives.

1

2

Unit 3, Listening and speaking Ex 6 page 77

1 Read this part of the quesionnaire and answer the questions. 2 Answer student A's questions.
3 Ask student A the questions on this page and make a note of his / her answers.

How vain are you?

1 Have you ever considered plastic surgery?
  a No, never
  b Yes, but only anti-ageing treatments when I get older
  c Yes, I am considering it at the moment
2 When you are going on holiday, do you plan your outfits beforehand?
  a No, I just throw everything in a suitcase
  b No, but I try to pick my favourite items
  c Yes, I always plan exactly what will go with each item
3 How often do you get your hair cut?
  a Never – I cut it myself b Once every 2 or 3 months
  c Every 6 weeks
4 How often do you buy fashion magazines?
  a Never. They are a waste of money
  b Sometimes. But I like ones that are not just fashion
  c Often. I buy lots of different ones
5 How many times do you look at yourself in the mirror every day?
  a 3 times or less b 4–10 times c More than 10 times

4 Compare your answers. If your answers are mainly 'a' you aren't at all vain. If your answers are mainly 'b' you are quite vain, but this is normal. If your answers are mainly 'c' you are too vain!